"From beginning to end, this volume has t[...] tion, the voice of a poet who knows exactly what he wants to say and how to say it. . . . Behind the range of styles and approaches, one recognizes a single honest and contemporary voice."—DANA GIOIA, *Poetry*

"[*After the Rain*] offers proof that the art of poetry is alive and well in America."—ROBERT PHILLIPS, *Houston Post*

"Everywhere one looks there are filaments of connection: to those who have gone before, elders, neighbors, laboring men, loved ones; to place, to past, to the earth itself. These are loving poems, delivered in a quiet, authoritative voice; the reader slips into their flow and partakes of a communion. . . . [This] is a remarkable achievement." —BRUCE BENNETT, *New York Times Book Review*

"[Jared Carter is] a poet thoroughly in the American grain. . . . *After the Rain* has a metaphysical complexity entirely in keeping with its great Shaker virtues of simplicity, clean line, and practical design." —ROBERT HOSMER, *Southern Review*

"Carter's is a poetry of a resolute middle distance, firmly of this world: between the dust under the earth and the dust of space there exists the place that the poem can illumine."—HELEN VENDLER, *New York Review of Books*

"[Carter] writes American poetry the way that William Faulkner wrote American novels. . . . [Carter's poems] have the homespun flavor of our native music—ballads, country blues, and sweet, clear, understated lyrics."—SALLY A. LODGE, *Publishers Weekly*

DARKENED ROOMS OF SUMMER

TED KOOSER CONTEMPORARY POETRY | *Editor:* Ted Kooser

.

DARKENED ROOMS OF SUMMER

New and Selected Poems

Jared Carter

Introduction by Ted Kooser

UNIVERSITY OF NEBRASKA PRESS | LINCOLN AND LONDON

Acknowledgments for the use of
copyrighted material appear on
pages xiii–xiv, which constitute an
extension of the copyright page.

Publication of this volume was made
possible in part by the generous
support of the H. Lee and Carol
Gendler Charitable Fund.

Library of Congress
Cataloging-in-Publication Data
Carter, Jared.
[Poems. Selections]
Darkened Rooms of Summer:
New and Selected Poems /
Jared Carter; Introduction
by Ted Kooser.
pages cm.—(Ted Kooser
Contemporary Poetry)
ISBN 978-0-8032-4857-1 (paper:
alk. paper)
ISBN 978-0-8032-5349-0 (pdf)
ISBN 978-0-8032-5385-8 (epub)
ISBN 978-0-8032-5400-8 (mobi)
I. Kooser, Ted. II. Title.
PS3553.A7812A6 2014
811'.54—dc23   2013034290

Set in Ehrhardt Pro
by Laura Wellington.
Designed by A. Shahan.

For Candace,
Tutilo, Elisabeth,
and Robert

I remember the days, the hours, the books, the seasons, the winter skies and darkened rooms of summer.

HENRY JAMES

Contents

From *Cross this Bridge at a Walk* | 2006

From *A Dance in the Street* | 2012

New Poems

Acknowledgments

Poems selected from *Work, for the Night Is Coming* are reprinted by permission of Jared Carter.

Author and publisher express their thanks to the Permissions Company, Inc., on behalf of the Cleveland State University Poetry Center (http://www.csuohio.edu/poetrycenter) for permission to reprint the following poems from *After the Rain* (copyright © 1993 by Jared Carter): "After the Rain," "Barn Siding," "The Believers," "Cecropia Moth," "Changeling," "Cicadas," "Drawing the Antique," "For an Old Flame," "For Starr Atkinson, Who Designed Books," "Foundling," "Galleynipper," "The Gleaning," "Interview," "Mississinewa Reservoir at Winter Pool," "Mourning Doves," "Phoenix," "Poem Written on a Line from *The Walam Olum*," "Portrait Studio," "The Purpose of Poetry," "Scryer," "Seed Storm," and "The Shriving," and from *Les Barricades Mystérieuses* (copyright © 1999 by Jared Carter): "Berceuse," "Candle," "Cemetery," "Clavichord," "Comet," "Ditchweed," "Ford," "Hawkmoth," "Improvisation," "Interlude," "Labyrinth," "Linen," "Millefiori," "Palimpsest," "Phosphorescence," "Reprise," "Summons," and "Tankroom." And thanks to Wind Publications, of Nicholasville, Kentucky, for permission to reprint poems from *Cross this Bridge at a Walk* and *A Dance in the Street*.

The author is grateful to print and online editors in whose publications the reprinted poems in this volume—sometimes in different versions and with different titles—originally appeared.

The selected poems were first published in *Backcountry, Barnwood Press Cooperative, Chronicles, The Chowder Review, Cumberland Poetry Review, Curriculum Vitae, Defined Providence, The Devil's Millhopper, Eclectica, Evansville Review, Fennel Stalk, The Formalist, Green's Magazine, The Harbor Review, Images, Indianapolis Journal, The Iowa Review, Kansas Quarterly, The Kenyon Review, The Laurel Review, The Long Story, Melic Review, Midwest Quarterly, Milkweed Quarterly, Mississippi Valley Review, Mockingbird, The Nation, New Letters, New Virginia Review, New Yorker, North Dakota Quarterly, Outposts, Poetry Quarterly, Pembroke Magazine,*

Pemmican, Pennsylvania Review, People's Culture, The Pikestaff Forum, Pivot, Plains Poetry Journal, Poetry, Prairie Schooner, Pteranodon, Published Poet Newsletter, Purdue University Perspective, The Reaper, The Scream Online, South Carolina Review, Sou'wester, Sparrow, TriQuarterly, Valparaiso Poetry Review, Wind/Literary Journal, Yarrow, Zone 3.

Thanks also to the editors of the following journals in which the new poems were first published: *At the Edge of the Prairie*: "Clouds," "Homestead"; *Blast Furnace*: "Torc"; *Eclectica Magazine*: "Dryad," "Schoolhouse"; *Galway Review*: "Achilles," "Ariadne," "Boleyn," "Graveyard," "Mourning," "Perseus," "Philoctetes," "Poetry," "Polyxena"; *Lucid Rhythms*: "Etruria"; *Shadow Road Quarterly*: "Moth," "Visitor"; *Shatter-Colors Literary Review*: "Adultery," "Cross-harp," "Priestess," "Vow"; *The New Formalist*: "Gone"; *Think Journal*: "Question"; *Trinacria*: "Awakening," "Prescription"; *Town Creek Poetry*: "Web"; *Valparaiso Poetry Review*: "Journeyman," "Treadwheel"; *Victorian Violet*: "Evergreen," "Twilight."

I have very little patience for long scholarly introductions, which are often so boring that it's difficult to have faith that something interesting may follow, and I usually skip over them without the least twinge of guilt. I wouldn't want these words of mine to stand as any kind of an obstacle on your way toward the rich poetry to follow, which you'll find to be far more moving and engaging than any professional literary opinion I might roll onto your path. Voltaire once said that opinion had caused more trouble on the earth than plagues and earthquakes, and I'm grateful to Voltaire for that. But there are a few things I do want to tell you about this book, which I admire and love.

Several years ago I asked the University of Nebraska Press if every couple of years they would permit me to introduce a significant selection of poems from the life work of a writer whose work, I felt, deserved more attention. Though I was proposing a series of books to be published occasionally, I had only one collection in mind at the time, and you're holding it now. My first objective in approaching the press was to entice their editors to share my enthusiasm for the remarkably fine poems of Jared Carter, which I had been reading with pleasure, admiration, and jealousy for almost forty years. Other important collections of verse will follow in due course, and I am pledged to that effort, but this is the book that's rightly and justly in the lead. And its publication coincides with the poet's seventy-fifth birthday, a fine occasion for a celebration like this.

A few words about the poet: Jared Carter was born in the town of Elwood, Indiana. His father was a general contractor, his neighbors were carpenters, seamstresses, housepainters, preachers, grave-diggers, cooks, and mechanics, working-class people with working-class lives and stories. And though Carter was to attend Yale and Goddard, to work as a journalist and in publishing, and eventually to become a distinguished member of the national literary community, everything he has published does honor to the good, well-intentioned people he grew up among. This poet doesn't merely write about his people, he writes for them, with affection and honesty, without an ounce of condescension. You'll find many poems in this book that you can push under the noses of people who say they don't like poetry, and they'll discover that they do like poetry, after all, and to their surprise will admit to liking it quite a lot. Sophisticated and artful as all of Carter's poems are, they are never, by his stated intention, beyond the reach of nonprofessional readers.

His first collection of poems, *Work, for the Night Is Coming*, won the prestigious Walt Whitman Award when Carter was forty-one, and he has gone on to publish a number of justly praised chapbooks and full-length collections during the subsequent years. He's been awarded National Endowment and Guggenheim Fellowships among a number of other distinctions. Individual poems have appeared in the *New Yorker*, *Poetry*, *Tri-Quarterly*, and in many other distinguished journals. But not enough readers know the beauty and emotion his work has to offer.

And skill. This poet can employ the most difficult of literary forms with such remarkable ease and grace that you won't even notice the scaffolding. He can tell a compelling story on the wings of authentic speech. He has said that his principal objective as a writer is to reach us with his poems, to move us, to touch our hearts. He calls our attention to things within our reach that it seems we've never noticed. He has been called a "preservationist poet" because he wants to preserve what he knows and loves, and he does that for us in an unforgettable, inimitable way.

It has been my great pleasure and privilege to encourage him to assemble a number of his earlier books here, and to include a selection of new work. The importance of *Darkened Rooms of Summer* will not derive from its place in American literature, where it shall earn the respect of scholars and critics for years to come, but from its place in the hearts of the broad audience that it will surely find. You'll want to loan this book to your friends and neighbors, but be sure to put your name somewhere inside because you're going to have to prove it's yours when you want to get it back.

DARKENED ROOMS OF SUMMER

From *Work, for the Night Is Coming* | 1981

Geodes

They are useless, there is nothing
to be done with them, no reason, only

the finding: letting myself down holding
to ironwood and the dry bristle of roots

into the creek bed, into clear water shelved
below the outcroppings, where crawdads spurt

through silt; clawing them out of clay, scrubbing
away the sand, setting them in a shaft of light

to dry. Sweat clings in the cliff's downdraft.
I take each one up like a safecracker listening

for the lapse within, the moment crystal turns
on crystal. It is all waiting there in darkness.

I want to know only that things gather themselves
with great patience, that they do this forever.

Early Warning

When the weather turned,
crows settled about the house,
cawing daylong among the new leaves.
It would be hard spring,
folks said, the crows—
they know. There are folks
up near where I come from
in Mississinewa County
who study such things.
Folks who believe tornadoes
are alive: that polluted streams
rise from their beds
like lepers, following after
some great churning, twisting cloud.
With their own eyes
they've seen a cyclone stop,
lap up electricity
from a substation, then make
a right-angle turn
and peel the roof off some
prefabricated egg factory.
Thousands of hens, who've never seen
the light of the sun, or
touched earth with their beaks,
go up the funnel like souls to God.

For Jack Chatham

For Jack Chatham, and his brother, Tom,
both without helmets, their red hair
streaming behind them in the wind.
For all those who rode big Harleys
and Indians back in the fifties,
who dropped out of school, of work,
of everything, to drive again and
again down the dark cylinders of air.
For Jack on that bright day hitting
the slick on the bridge and landing
exactly in the center of Fall Creek
so that coroners from adjoining counties
argued over his body while the deputies
took Tom down the road to a place
where the Klan hung out and bought him
a few beers and patted him on the ass
saying it's all right, kid—
go on riding while you got the chance.

The Madhouse

I cannot give you the squeak
of the blue chalk on the cue tip,
the sound of the break, or the movement
about the table, like a ritual of wine;

then I was not born. My father,
who saw it, was still in high school;
and there are others who remember
the poolroom on the avenue.

Here lounged the former heroes
of the high-school team, who took
the Tri-State Crown in '24, and tied
with Massillon in '25. Catholics all,

a backfield composed of Swede
Svendson at fullback, the Baxter brothers
at either half, and handsome Richard
O'Reilly at the quarter.

They had no peers, then or now.
On Saturdays regularly they stood,
hats firmly on their heads, watching
the procession of hooded Klansmen

coming up Anderson Street, heading
toward the Main intersection. Always
the Klan demanded hats removed
before the flag they carried,

always the boys at the Madhouse refused,
and began unscrewing the weighted ends
of their pool cues. People came to watch;
the police stood apart; the Klan

never got past the Madhouse. That
was years ago. They're all dead now,
Swede and the Baxter boys, and
handsome Richard O'Reilly,

who married the banker's daughter;
and the Klansmen too. Only the men
who were boys then can still remember.
They talk about it, even now,

sitting in Joe's barbershop
watching cars go by, or sipping a beer
in Condon's tavern. It is a story
I heard when I was a boy. Lately

there's been a doughnut shop
where the Madhouse used to stand.
Mornings when I stop for coffee
I can almost hear it: the nine ball

dropping in the corner pocket,
the twelve rolling to within an inch
of the side; voices in the street
echoing along the store-fronts.

Walking the Ties

This was the old woman who ate canned dog food
this the red wagon she pulled through the alleys
this the pack of stray dogs that went with her

Here are the boys who shouted and threw things
here are the barrels of trash they all searched through
here are the boys' dogs barking at the old woman's dogs

There is the bar where she went each night to sit
there is the sparkling SCHLITZ sign over the mirror
there is the jukebox that only works if you kick it

These are the sleeves she touched each night when she left
these are the dogs coming out of the shadows to join her
these are the ties of the railroad tracks home

Yes
these are the ties of the railroad tracks home

Glacier

Last night I saw it form again
along the woods' dark edge;
heard it gathering out of a wind
from the northwest. Cornflowers
bent to the earth in its wake,
animals delved in their burrows,
leaves stiffened and fell.
I searched through the grass
for a stone scratched by ice,
but could not read its markings
in the faltering light. Found
another stone smoothed by water,
opened it to a page of wings.
Lastly an arrowhead. Left
all these things together
in a level field, to be kept
by snow, and raised high or low.

Mississinewa County Road

When you drive at dusk, alone,
after the corn is harvested, the wind
scatters bits of dry husk along the road.
A farmer has draped a groundhog's carcass
across the corner of a wire fence
and the crows have pecked out its eyes.
Your headlights show these things
to a part of your mind that cannot hurry,
that has never learned to decide.
While the car goes on, you get out
and stand, with the chaff blowing,
and crickets in the grass at the road's edge.
In the distance there is a dog barking
and somewhere a windmill turning in the wind.

The Oddfellows' Waiting Room
at Glencove Cemetery

There must always be a place like this
where the dimensions collapse inwardly
like a telescope you slip into your pocket.
Always a building with gables and arched windows,

always the polished floorboards of quartersawn oak,
the ceremonial chairs, the lectern, the gavel—
everything made of oak, and oak outside and alive,
shading this gathering place, measuring light

falling through glass veins stained green and gold,
oak nodding with a slow breath of wind in the boughs.
If you could peer downward through this earth
with such clarity, there would be only dust;

if you could peer through the other end of things
there would be only dust, too. What light reveals
here, in this room, is the grain of the bare oak floor
and the shadows of leaves moving with the grain.

The Undertaker

Time came when Sefe Graybill, the undertaker—
the only bidder on moving three-hundred-odd graves
from the Mount Moriah churchyard to higher ground
before the Mississinewa began climbing its banks
to fill the new reservoir—could find no one
in the congregation, none of those helping each other
move their things out in trucks, who would work for him.

It all had to be dug by hand. Some of the graves
had been there a hundred years or more. He drove
through little towns farther north, stopped at taverns
across from filling stations, at crossroads cafés
where they still serve a noon plate lunch. Talked
with men who had dug graves, once, with pick and spade,
back before the war. Machines put them all out of work.

They had found other ways to live. Balding, gray, gone
in the belly, they still needed money. He took them
to the knoll by the covered bridge, paid by the grave.
Each man slowly recognized, like a combination of lost numbers,
that men younger than themselves had labored here,
grown old, and were gone, who had lifted this same earth,
who had put in what they now took out, trying not to look

Yet seeing all: that these were the old tools in their hands,
that the sod came up in broken strips, and was cold,
that each shaft found its own way into the darkness,
that even carpenters in those times knew what they built for,
choosing wood not for the end but the journey, that no jeweler
had lived among these people, that they had sought remembrance,
that the sun's arc changes with the passage of days.

Sefe could only walk among them, explaining what they saw:
this is a business like any other. Some he had not seen before—

when they brought up what they could find of Amos King,
who had served in the War of 1812, who had helped lay out
the township: an ironstone pipe, a bag of arrowheads,
a Sheffield steel knife. When they brought up his wife:
an ivory medallion of an elephant crushing a man.

Fell overcome with heat, one did, the first day;
another struck by the sun; two more threw down their tools
and walked away. The few who stayed till the job was done
rode together in the back of Sefe's pickup each quitting time
to a tavern on the highway, near where they parked.
No one else world go there then. Sat there drinking,
cursing Sefe, buying him drinks, swearing they could not last.

Monument City

How I came to that leaf-shadowed house by the river—
    late-summer afternoon rain falling long into evening—
to visit a favorite aunt, who had asked the undertaker—
    his blue pickup truck pulled off just under the willows—

To take photographs of the house, and the gardens,
    and the parlor—with us in it—one last time
before the waters began to rise, and scavengers came
    to pick over the buildings too big to be moved—

She had seen his truck parked all summer in the churchyard
    on the far side of the covered bridge, with a tent
pitched first over this headstone, then that, until
    he and his helpers had taken them all up again, like bulbs,

And planted them on higher ground, in a cemetery
    provided by the government. An old friend of his—
this woman with gray braids piled on top of her head,
    who had lived on the corner across from the monument

And taught school thirty-five years until consolidation.
    He still lived on the second floor of the funeral parlor
down at the crossing, that had been a feed store once,
    in his father's day. Had carried two wives

Out through those double doors, and a son, to the churchyard.
    He brought with him now a box camera on a wooden tripod
and sat with us there in the parlor till nightfall, waiting
    for the rain to stop, for there to be some light—

How I came to be there that time I cannot remember, only
    walking out to the flowers, at dusk, with the two of them,
into air fresh from rain, and thunder far away, to the east,
    and lightning that showed us a path through the tall grass.

Work, for the Night Is Coming

On the road out of town past the old quarry
I watched a light rain darkening ledges
blocked and carded by the drill's bit

twenty years back. Within those stiff lines,
places half-stained with damp, the rock face
opened to a deeper grain—the probable drift

of the entire ridge outlined for a moment
by the rain's discoloring. Then all turned dim—
grass holding to the seams, redbud scattered

across the cliff, dark pool of water
rimmed with broken stones, where rain, now
falling steadily, left no lasting pattern.

At the Sign-Painter's

Of them all—those laboring men who knew my first name
and called out to me as I watched them coming up the walk;
the ones with birthmarks and missing fingers and red hair,
who had worked for my grandfather, and now my father;
who had gone home to wash up and put on a clean shirt;
who came to the back door Friday evenings for their checks;
who drove a Ford coupe and had a second wife and three kids
and were headed for town to have a drink and buy groceries—

Of the ones too old to work—in their black shoes laced up
with hooks, and their string ties, who stood on the sidewalk
when we were building something, and asked my father
if he remembered the house-moving business back during
the Depression: how you squirmed through all that dust
and broken glass in the crawl space, nudging ten-by-twelves
twenty feet long, and lugged the house-jacks behind you
one at a time, setting them up just right. How you moved
on your back like a crab through darkness, cobwebs
brushing your face, an iron bar in your hands, a voice
calling from somewhere outside, asking for a quarter-turn—

Of them all—plumbers, tinners, roofers, well-diggers,
carpenters, cement finishers with their padded knees—
I liked the sign-painters best: liked being taken there
by my father, following after him, running my fingers
along the pipe railing, taking his hand as we climbed up
the concrete embankment to their back-street shop looking
out across the Nickel Plate yard—
                                    liked being left to wander
among piles of fresh pine planks, tables caked and smeared
and stacked with hundreds of bottles and jars leaking color
and fragrance, coffee cans jammed with dried brushes, skylight
peppered with dead flies, narrow paths that wound among
signs shrouded with tape and newspaper—all the way back

to the airshaft, the blackened sink, the two-burner hotplate,
spoons sticking from china mugs, behind the curtain the bed
with its torn army blanket—liked feeling beneath my toes
the wood floors patterned with forgotten colors, soft
to the step, darkened with grime and soot from the trains—

Liked them most of all—those solemn old men with skin
bleached and faded as their hair, white muslin caps
speckled with paint, knuckles and fingers faintly dotted—
liked them for their listening to him about the sign
he wanted painted, for pretending not to notice me watching—
for the wooden rod with its black knob resting lightly
against the primed surface, for the slow sweep and whisper
of the brush—liked seeing the ghost letters in pencil
gradually filling out, fresh and wet and gleaming, words
forming out of all that darkness, that huge disorder.

Turning the Brick

Men worked turning the brick
at the end of our street—
They gave each one a quarter-turn
and put it back again. That

was what the Depression was like
where I grew up. Each day
they got closer to our house;
everybody came out to watch.

They had their shirts off,
down on their knees—old scars
flared in the sunlight, tattoos
glistened on their arms. Men

with no teeth, with noses
turned and bent, fingers missing.
The bricks were tan-colored;
each had a picture on the bottom:

a scene of ships, a name, a date.
One of the men brushed the sand
from a brick and held it out.
We gathered around. He let us touch

the rough emblem, the letters,
the year. He gave the brick
a quarter-turn, put it back
in the street, and went on.

Landing the Bees

First the bough of the apple bending; neighbors
calling to one another in their watery voices,
none venturing close to the glittering branch.

They make way for the old bee man, in his felt hat,
who spreads a sheet on the grass, a white sheet
from his own bed, and with a pocket mirror

casts the sun's image up into the swarm.
If you have walked in sleep, you know this movement
out through air, through blossoming, down

to a new place, drawn by a brilliance in the leaves
and folded into whiteness. He takes them up
as though carrying coals. If you have wakened

arms outstretched, you know this moment: things
rising of their own accord are beckoning
to themselves. It is your own voice murmuring.

The Measuring

You're sickly pale—a crooked root,
but one last remedy remains:
before the dawn we'll go on foot
through grass sleeked down by heavy rains
to the sexton's house. Already he
takes down his spade, and goes
to walk among the whitened rows.
His wife awaits with lengths of string
necessary for measuring.

She has no fire alight, nor words
to spare, but bolts the wooden door
and helps you out of clothes that fall
soundlessly to the floor. Naked,
you mount the table and recline;
she comes, her eight stiff fingers
trailing bright bits of twine. First,
crown to nose, then mouth to chin,
pressing against each crevice, in
and down the length of your cold frame—
whispering unintelligible names.

The feet are last to stretch: from heel
to toe each one must be times seven
the other piece. She nods, and knots
the two together, breathes her spell,
then turns to go. I leave a pair
of silver dollars there, and take
the string to tie where it will rot
the winter long, on hinge of gate,
wheelbarrow shaft, or eaves-trough's fall.

Behind us, where the darkness drains,
a blackbird settles on the roof

and calls back to another that rain
is coming like an awful proof.
The two denounce the scratching sound
the sexton's spade makes on the ground—
measuring off the careful square
of someone else expected there.

Ginseng

A god-fearing man did not labor
on the Sabbath, or witch for water
during the week, or work charms
for warts or rain. When he told her
we were going to the bottomland
after Sunday dinner, it would be
to see if that oak limb had fallen yet
or whether the crows were in the corn.
The scythe would be hidden already
out by the gate, buried knee-deep
in Queen Anne's lace. We would sit
on the front-porch swing listening
to her read scripture, until bees
drifting about the clematis vine
made her drowsy. When she leaned
into sleep, he eased her body
against the cushions, and waved me
toward the gate.
                    I think we became
her dream: child with the same eyes
and silver hair as his, running bare-
footed; old man bent like the scythe
he carried—for no apparent reason,
no grass high enough there to mow,
the land swept clean by the glacier,
by ten thousand years of the creek
switching its tail back and forth,
and at least twenty head of cattle
grazing the last hundred.
                    Beyond
the pasture they had railed off
a branch of the creek for thistles
and jimsonweed. We walked there,
the scythe in my hands now, since

those who taught him had carried one
while looking for ginseng: something
to have with you at the first place
you come to, so that you may nod,
and pass by; something to lean on
when you find the right cluster
and stand looking down at it—
wondering how many dry-weight ounces
of root it would yield, how long
it has been growing there, who else
had harvested it since the Nanticoke
passed through here gathering things
before there were roads.
                                    Even now,
he explained, men dig it up, ruin
whole stands, steal it from farmers.
But all of them together—hunters,
thieves, those who keep the old ways—
pass it from hand to hand along
a chain of those who know exactly
where it is going, what it is worth—
until eventually it arrives
on the other side of the world,
where it is ground into dust
and mixed into potions they say
can make an old man young again.

Going back, he would let me carry
the scythe, to leave it hidden
once more in the weeds by the gate.
She would be up and waiting for us
by the well, and I would pump
while they splashed water on their faces.
When she awoke with the Book in her lap,
she said, and watched the two of us
coming across the ridge in the heat,
we seemed to shimmer, to step toward her

like two unexpected messengers
come from an old story. For a moment
she could even make out the cord
that bound us together—now long,
like an arm stretched between us,
now like a vein of lightning opening.

Shaking the Peonies

I would lie down again in your bed of fabrications
like a quilt of many voices covering me in darkness—
colors stitched from the motions of your hands bringing water
from low places, or your kneeling each morning to build a fire,
as though the sun had come to call, and we were all new.

I would sit peeling apples with you in the plum-tree shade,
waiting for the four-o'clocks to open. When the dog
found his corner at bedtime, I would again watch his turning,
hear your voice, and see immemorial grasses bending.
When you asked, the longlegs pointed the way of the wind;
when you put the shell to my ear, I heard the sea.

I would go again with you carrying cans of bright flowers,
heavy iron shears, sun hats made of straw, and gloves—
peonies falling over drowsy to the ground by that day
and gathered in bunches ivory and white, like girls
gowned in green leaves. I would imitate your swinging
as you show me how to shake off the ants, and they fall.

Go following after you on that day of light and stones
lodged in a green meadow: to place the blades of grass again
in order, to trace the hard insignia of hearts, smooth links
of chain, and tools; to be again there with you encountering
old friends, who also come to decorate each year, who speak
of times when you were young together. Listening to voices

admiring the flame of blossoms, the bees, the white lamb
that waits on the stone: would hear pollen in those shadows—
all the naming, gathering of things, parts innumerable
that make up this world. There I would lie down again, yes
and become whole, like the ending of a story, and sleep.

Birdstone

Of the traditional priestly tasks,
the offices carried out by the elders,
the secrets entrusted: the birdstone
bears these in its beak like a slate feather.

No one touches this feather, it is a song
my grandfather taught me for twirling
the fire-bow, for hewing the ax-head,
for weaving the platform of nettles.

When the last breath goes out of a man
he must wait above the earth in the sun
and the rain until the old songs leave him
like smoke, like a plume blown by the wind.

When I die finally and you bind it
against my wrinkled forehead
the birdstone will confirm all this for you
and brush your lips, once, with its stiff wings.

From *After the Rain* | 1993

After the Rain

After the rain, it's time to walk the field
again, near where the river bends. Each year
I come to look for what this place will yield—
lost things still rising here.

The farmer's plow turns over, without fail,
a crop of arrowheads, but where or why
they fall is hard to say. They seem, like hail,
dropped from an empty sky,

Yet for an hour or two, after the rain
has washed away the dusty afterbirth
of their return, a few will show up plain
on the reopened earth.

Still, even these are hard to see—
at first they look like any other stone.
The trick to finding them is not to be
too sure about what's known;

Conviction's liable to say straight off
this one's a leaf, or that one's merely clay,
and miss the point: after the rain, soft
furrows show one way

Across the field, but what is hidden here
requires a different view—the glance of one
not looking straight ahead, who in the clear
light of the morning sun

Simply keeps wandering across the rows,
letting his own perspective change.
After the rain, perhaps, something will show,
glittering and strange.

Phoenix

Right from Merom on State Road 63 to the junction
with the Mann Cemetery Road. ... Here are buried
two of General Harrison's soldiers, Kentuckians who
carried an old family feud into the army and killed
each other on the way to the Battle of Tippecanoe.
    At 5.3 *m* is the junction ... Graysville Road ...
50 yards L. of the bridge is the BIG SPRING where
General Harrison's expeditionary army camped the
night of September 29, 1811.
    It was at this spring that the two soldiers from
Kentucky slew each other. The waters of the spring
are caught now in a moss-covered brick enclosure.
Indiana: A Guide to the Hoosier State

He knew. They all knew, there was no use
pretending. The Shawnees knew. We knew
they were out there. They knew we were
coming. Everybody knew. We all knew why.

Why didn't he and I fight and be done with it?
Why did we bother to join up, put on those coats
with the strange buttons, why did we drill
and march, side by side, but never speak?

The General knew, and we knew. That evening
when he sent the two of us down to the spring,
and told us to leave our rifles behind,
we understood. At the bottom of that hollow,

beneath a limestone ledge, a dark presence
rose up—a basin of troubled water, seething
and boiling, surging over heaps of stones,
catching the last light through the trees—

and after a while, when we had filled
all the canteens, one by one, both of us
kneeling there, reaching into the depths,
our fingers gone half numb—there were no

clear reflections, only the broken heave
of light and dark, and it seemed as though
that motion had found its way inside me,
and I knew we could put it off no longer.

We had come all this way, with the Shawnees
waiting for us. They were out there now,
watching. I couldn't risk their taking him;
somehow he belonged to me, and me to him.

I drew my skinning knife and looked across
and saw him crouched there with his dagger.
We stumbled through the shallows, smashing
against each other like a pair of rams.

His blade burned deep in my right side
but I knew the spring would cool the pain
and soon I would be free of an old anger,
the resentment I had carried for so long.

I shoved my knife clear to the hilt up
inside him, and stood for a moment lifting
with both hands, holding him on its point,
before he fell away, taking me with him,

out onto the pool. From where we landed,
tangled in each other's arms, neither of us
had the strength to move. We lay gasping;
dark plumes began to spread out around us.

I could not feel the water's coldness.
I struggled, trying to push him away,

but he clung fast. I took a deep breath
and found I could still speak. I said

his name—it was my father's middle name,
and he stirred, as though hearing someone
calling from a long way off. His eyelids
fluttered, and I decided to talk to him,

to let him know I was still there. I tried
to make the sound of my own voice rise up
above the gurgle of the spring. I told him
he had my father's middle name. I recited

the names of my sisters, brothers, aunts,
uncles, my mother. I said my mother's name
again. There was no reply. He came closer,
his face half out of the troubled surface.

I told him the names of our hunting dogs,
and our horse, and the horse before that.
I told him I thought night would come soon.
Finally I began to tell him what Bob Petty,

the old schoolmaster, had explained to me
just the day before—about the creature
with outstretched wings, the bird stamped
on the ormolu buttons of our uniforms.

I told him what Petty had said: those coats
were originally designed for Napoleon,
for the soldiers in his army, for when
he finished with Europe, and got ready

to come over to America. Those uniforms
were stored in a warehouse somewhere
down in New Orleans. But then Napoleon
sold everything west of the Mississippi

to Tom Jefferson, and the uniforms got
left behind when the French pulled out.
General Harrison had heard about them,
and bought them cheap, for this campaign.

All that time, on the march from Vincennes,
we had touched these strange buttons, morning
and night, but never known. I went on talking,
there in the twilight, in case he was listening.

What can you do with a man who insists on
stealing away, while you cling to the edge
of an endless flow, but still have something
important to say? My voice was a whisper now.

The bird was called a phoenix—a creature
that would never die, that built its nest
in fire, and rose up from its own ashes.
It could sleep, Petty said, on the waves

of the sea, even in the midst of a storm.
I came to the end, but he no longer seemed
to care. This time, when he drifted off,
I let him go, out toward the deepest part.

A darkness had spread over the spring,
but I hung on to the moss and boulders
there at the edge, and by the last light
I watched the water all turn clear again.

The Gleaning

All day long they have been threshing
and something breaks: the canvas belt
that drives the separator flies off,
parts explode through the swirl
of smoke and chaff, and he is dead
where he stands—drops the pitchfork
as they turn to look at him—and falls.
They carry him to the house and go on
with the work. Five wagons and their teams
stand waiting, it is still daylight,
there will be time enough for grieving.

When the undertaker comes from town
he brings the barber, who must wait
till the women finish washing the body.
Neighbors arrive from the next farm
to take the children. The machines
shut down, one by one, horses
are led away, the air grows still
and empty, then begins to fill up
with the sounds of cicada and mourning dove.
The men stand along the porch, talking
in low voices, smoking their cigarettes;
the undertaker sits in the kitchen
with the family.
                      In the parlor
the barber throws back the curtains
and talks to this man, whom he has known
all his life, since they were boys
together. As he works up a lather
and brushes it onto his cheeks,
he tells him the latest joke. He strops
the razor, tests it against his thumb,
and scolds him for not being more careful.
Then with darkness coming over the room

he lights a lamp, and begins to scrape
at the curve of the throat, tilting the head
this way and that, stretching the skin,
flinging the soap into a basin, gradually
leaving the face glistening and smooth.

And as though his friend had fallen asleep
and it were time now for him to stand up
and stretch his arms, and look at his face
in the mirror, and feel the closeness
of the shave, and marvel at his dreaming—
the barber trims the lamp, and leans down,
and says, for a last time, his name.

Scryer

The first time when I was thirteen mother
came into my room that night saying there
there you've been dreaming it's only a bad

dream but I could still see a strange light
everywhere, horses banging against the stalls,
my father and brothers running, calling out

it's only a dream she said now go to sleep.
Next morning I told them but no one listened,
no one remembered three weeks later when

the barn burned to the ground though they
managed to save the horses. The second time
I was fourteen and told no one I had seen

a neighbor drifting face down in the river,
there there go to sleep it's only a dream.
I stood and wept the day they buried him

though no one knew why—stood praying
in the churchyard let there be no third time,
I could not bear to look into that stream again,

that dark shining, let no one hear or remember
what I dream in the night. But the preacher heard,
and knew I would not tell, and took me away,

down to the river. When he had finished
he gave me a ring with a crystal stone
and I looked in its heart and fell asleep

and knew it was not horses or men I saw into
but fire turned hard as ice, and brimming with light
and a voice in the night saying there there

The Shriving

And the seventh angel poured out his vial into the air.

Revelation 16:17

He was a druggist. The storefront building
had one long room with a pressed-tin ceiling,
a line of revolving fans down the middle,
and random-oak floors darkened with polishing.
The soda-fountain counter was a slab
of black glass chipped with tiny moons.
There were tables and chairs made of wire
where you brought your date after a game:
you could look up and see yourself in the mirror.
The boys who worked there had imported brooms
with handles maybe ten feet long or more;
once each week they had to sweep the ceiling.
When the brooms wore out, the druggist took them,
saved them for a time when he burnt the worms.

Save for the times when he burnt the worms,
I never saw him smile. If those who lived there
had a name for sacred, they never said it aloud.
Once when I was small the aunties took me out
to a grove of walnut trees with nothing else
around them, no green thing strong enough
to rise up from that ground. Some called it
poison, others spoke of a strange power
in the earth itself, which the tree could summon.
My morning there, gathering nuts—black
clinkers—stained my fingers for weeks after.
And from my first glimpse of that place I knew
there are some things not written in books,
there are some trees whose names you know on sight.

These are the names of the trees I came to know:
willow, which is first to turn green in springtime,
poplar, which looks silver when the wind blows,
oak, which is always last to let go of its leaves.
Each time he turned the car into the lane
he praised the walnut trees that stood there:
how they would bring a fortune at the mill,
how their heartwood, sliced thin as paper,
would unfold like ripples in a stream.
But they were his possession now, they came
with the house; he aimed to see they lived out
their span. When the first tent-moths arrived
and spread their stickiness through the trees,
he began to sweat, to cry out in his sleep.

Those who talked in their sleep, who could not rest,
came to the store each day to visit the druggist,
waited in line for a chance to say what was wrong.
Wednesday afternoons he closed, like the bank,
and stayed in the back room, counting the stock.
He knew she would be lounging on the bedclothes,
talking to some drummer who stands by the door,
who wants a cigarette now but lacks the nerve
to light one up. She would tell about her husband,
how he killed moths and butterflies in a jar;
the man would begin pulling on his pants.
The druggist tilts a line of pills into a box,
tells the boys to be sure and sweep the ceiling,
he is going home now, there are chores to do.

Going home after practice, doing the chores—
those things kept me busy. When the war started
the state widened the road to four lanes,
chopped down the trees in front of his house.
But even before that, when he first retired,
and she was long dead, of some illness,
and I, his grand-nephew, was left there

on summer mornings, for him to look after—
even then I guessed at what had happened:
when he would gather up the old tools
and get a worn-out broom down from the loft
and go out to burn the caterpillar nests
where they clotted the trees. When I watched him
make harsh changes in the way things were.

Change made him harsh. Things got in the way
of what he saw and heard. It took a long time
for him to tie the rags about the broom,
soak them in fuel oil, then strike a match
and hoist the fuming torch into the air,
touching it here and there among the leaves
where moths were dreaming. I saw them burst
and fall in a bright rain against the grass.
And when the trees were purged, and he stood
with hair and eyebrows full of soot, calling,
pointing toward the branches above, saying how
they were safe now, the fire had healed them,
and when I grew up, I could do it too—
I knew she was not dead, she had run away.

I learned one does not run away from death:
it comes like a harsh glare billowing darkness.
When I went back, after the war, and stopped
at the café next to the bank, no one there
remembered me, though they recalled his name.
"He drove his car onto the tracks one night,"
a farmer said. "Those Nickel Plate tracks
are gone now, all the way to Windfall.
You can hunt rabbit on the old right-of-way
and not worry about some train hitting you.
That whole stretch has come up in wild cherry;
last year the trees were thick with moths."
"I remember him now," the feed store man said.
"He was a druggist. Had a storefront building."

39

Mississinewa Reservoir at Winter Pool

A reservoir's not like a lake;
it depends on how much water's
coming in. When it goes down,
in the fall, you can see where

the town used to be—brick
foundations, chunks of concrete,
things still not worn away.
Sunday afternoons in October

the people who lived there once
come back, drive their cars
down to where the road breaks off.
They walk out toward the river.

Nothing remains. The walls of the houses
are gone, the school, the church.
There are no flowers, no trees;
even the cemetery has been moved.

And yet they have come home again,
nothing can harm them now.
They walk to and fro, stopping
to speak, nodding, as though

having risen from a deep sleep
and come at last to a place
no longer having anything in it
except themselves. And as though always.

The Purpose of Poetry

This old man grazed thirty head of cattle
in a valley just north of the covered bridge
on the Mississinewa, where the reservoir
stands today. Had a black border collie
and a half-breed sheep dog with one eye.
The dogs took the cows to pasture each morning
and brought them home again at night
and herded them into the barn. The old man
would slip a wooden bar across both doors.
One dog slept on the front porch, one on the back.

He was waiting there one evening
listening to the animals coming home
when a man from the courthouse stopped
to tell him how the new reservoir
was going to flood all his property.
They both knew he was too far up in years
to farm anywhere else. He had a daughter
who lived in Florida, in a trailer park.
He should sell now and go stay with her.
The man helped bar the doors before he left.

He had only known dirt under his fingernails
and trips to town on Saturday mornings
since he was a boy. Always he had been around
cattle, and trees, and land near the river.
Evenings by the barn he could hear the dogs
talking to each other as they brought in
the herd, and the cows answering them.
It was the clearest thing he knew. That night
he shot both dogs and then himself.
The purpose of poetry is to tell us about life.

Poem Written on a Line from the *Walam Olum*

There at the edge of all the water where the land ends ...

I was not certain she would meet me there.
Go first and wait, she said, down at the edge
below the bend, where the road forks, and all
the cattails are brown and blown, and water
backed up in the creek makes a dark land
where no one ever goes. You'll see both ends

of a caved-in barn on the left. The property ends
at the barbed wire, but go on from there—
look for a path through the marsh, to higher land
where you come out in cottonwoods, and the edge
of the bluff where you stand shows dark water
moving so slowly it seems not to move at all.

This mound was where the village stood, and all
you see from here, she said, to the far ends
of the clearing, they built up from the water
passing below us now. The mussels down there
were edible then, and at the river's edge
they cracked the shells and tossed them on the land.

She had come up to stand beside me. Island,
really, she said, when the rains come, and all
the lowlands flood. No way to get an edge
on anything here. When the grant money ends
I'll go back to the college. Nothing there,
I'll tell them, nothing near that dark water

worth digging for. They've flown over water
from here to the Ohio, they think the land
can't hide a single site from them. There

should be places people can't find at all.
She folded up her shirt, unhooked the ends
that held her bra, and stepped back through the edge

of shade beneath the trees. A thinner edge
of sunlight showed her body like whitewater
gleaming. Nothing done well ever ends,
she said, touching my hand, not even land
built up one act at a time, so that all
that went before, and after, still waits there.

Then there was movement, as though the land
were water, without edge or ends, and all
I hoped to find or know was gathering there.

Foundling

I would be safe there; she would look after me now.
When the car drove off, she showed me sweet alyssum
growing among the flagstones, and called it with names
learned from her own grandmother—madwort, heal-bite,
gold-dust, basket-of-gold. In the house, in the room
with the oak cupboard, I would have my own bed. Later,
when company came, and they thought I had fallen asleep,
I heard them speak of a love child in the neighborhood,
whose parents had gone away. I wanted to comfort it—
longed to call out to them that I would be its mother.

Next morning she made cinnamon toast and cambric tea.
They had invited me to visit them all. I ran across
to the house of the two doctors—father and daughter,
homeopathic practitioners—who promised to fetch me
on their trips through the woods, who said I could carry
their long-handled baskets, and help pick hibiscus
and lemon grass, and seek out charms for bee sting
and balm for sunburn—but they were gone already,
in the morning cool, searching along the riverbank.
No one remained who could tell me how love had children.

Next, to the widow's house, by the water's edge,
to wait on the screened-in porch for their return,
finding a place to sit among stacks of magazines,
watching her trim strawflowers to bind for drying,
saying aloud the words she taught me—immortelle
and everlasting—and going out to her garden full
of unfading things: helping her gather up armloads
of ruby and amber cockscomb, stripping the leaves
from the stalks, bringing them back to the porch
to hang in great rippled bunches, dusky and velvet.

I heard them singing harmony, coming along the path.
When I asked, none of them knew where the love child
had gone, but all affirmed I had not been dreaming.
We are children of nature, they said, therefore of love;
we rise up perennial, like tansy, or heartsease, or phlox,
some meant for healing, others for beauty. Our lasting
is seasonal, takes time, becomes life itself, is love.
All that autumn, they said, I could watch the cockscomb
giving itself away in seeds that fell to the newspaper.
Each day I could write my name in its last, best gift.

Over the years I grew and prospered in that green place
always shining with light from the river, that world
that is gone now, under the waters, and can never return.
During the day I was joined with their stories; and once,
during feigned sleep, I heard those same voices whisper
the names of my real mother and father, who loved each other,
who left their mark on my own flesh, as one might draw
letters in the sandbank of a stream, or a fresh snowfall.
Over the years I remember the willows shading those walkways,
the gardens we tended, the flowers we gave to each other.

Barn Siding

It can fetch a dollar a board foot
with the right customer, but I've seen
all the old barns I'm going to mess with
for a while. Got no more need for them.

There's no reason for a man my age
taking risks. Time to pay attention
to what's happened in your life, maybe
pass it along to someone younger.

I never got past eighth grade. Never
worked inside, or had to wear a tie,
or sat at a desk. Learned what I know
the hard way. It helps you remember.

When you get in trouble is when you
start to forget. It happened to me,
looking for barnwood. I got greedy,
forgot what I had learned years before:

if you're putting up kiln-dried lumber
and something starts to crack or splinter,
you've got time to get out of the way;
but old wood won't give any warning.

You take a barn or farmhouse that's stood
a hundred years or more, it's had time
to gravitate, work out all the stress.
That wood's cured; got no more surprises.

Tamper with that balance, and you've got
problems. A house will talk to itself
when the sun hits it, or a cold wind;
it tries to adjust. You've got to hear.

That's what you need in this business: ears.
A picker's always going in places
where he shouldn't be. Has to listen,
know when something's about to happen.

What does a picker do? Picks over
what other people have left behind.
Attics. Basements. Sheds. Like this old place
I knew about in Prophet Township.

There was a woods around it. The bridge
a mile up the road had been out
for years. Nobody came along there
anymore. I kept an eye on it

for a long time. I let others have
first choice. Couples from town like to park
along country lanes. Boys with rifles
come shoot out all the windows. Hoboes,

people who start fires. Old house burns
in a place that far out, no one comes.
Maybe you look across the fields some night,
see a red glow way off in the sky.

I heard the barn didn't burn. Gave it
a few more years, let the new trees get
a toehold. Let the grapevines grow thick.
Then one day I drove out there to see.

What you're looking for is siding with
no color, it's just gone natural
from all that weather. Sometimes the nails
have rusted clear through. You can pry off

big long, smooth pieces with your bare hands.
It's dry, and limber, like old leather

that's been cured right. Every board has what
interior decorators call

"character." If you had gotten up
before daylight and gone out to milk
half a dozen cows, day in, day out
for thirty-odd years, you might call it

something else. But it doesn't matter.
Most of that wood turns out to be pine,
it's full of knots and scattered nail holes,
places where rust has darkened the grain.

I'd been out there all day by myself,
tromping a path through the grass and weeds,
had half a load of tongue-and-groove boards
stacked in the pick-up. Stopped now and then

to try the raspberries growing wild
right up to the double doors. No one
living on that place for thirty years,
limestone chimney where the house had been.

I kept on working. Late afternoon
I took a pair of gloves and a pry-bar
and climbed all the way up to the loft.
Half the floorboards weren't even nailed down.

I fixed up a place to slide them out
a window, took it slow, dropped one plank
at a time down onto the horseweeds.
I'd been up there maybe half an hour,

thought I saw something move. Didn't hear
a thing, just noticed this shadow drift
across the north wall. Sometimes you freeze
before you've had time to think: maybe

it's a mud-dauber hanging there near
your face. Other times your body knows,
takes over, goes where it wants to go,
always brings you out the quickest way.

Even so, I've wondered why that barn
made no noise at all: queen posts starting
to fold in on themselves, rafters, joists,
all those cedar shakes, tons of dry wood

held together for a hundred years,
all beginning to boil, like a storm
brewing, but no thunder, no more sound
than wind making circles in the grass.

I like to think there was nothing left
that could speak, except the wood itself,
everything else was already gone—
grain bin empty, all the old harness

stolen, someone had even climbed up
on the roof to get the lightning rods.
That kind of rod held a big glass ball
people used to say would turn sky blue

from all the current running through it.
You've walked through old houses, or places
that have burnt: nothing but broken cups,
bits of glass, corncobs, heaps of ashes.

Makes you wonder why people would up
and leave a place like that. What happened,
why nobody can make the land pay,
why it all comes up in second growth.

All you hear are stories. This family
tried and lost, that man wore himself out,

this man went out to the barn during
the sale, put a shotgun in his mouth.

You never know why. And there's never
anyone left to tell by the time
some picker stops by to have a look;
there's usually nothing left at all.

There was nothing on this place except
the barn, and nothing left in the barn
except the wood. It had been there all
that time, waiting for the right moment.

Something was holding it together,
some old balance, but when I got down
and pried up that last board, and pushed it
over the edge, the balance was gone

and the whole building simply started
turning itself inside out. The barn
was spiked, and here and there the rain had
gotten in, and turned those handmade nails

to rust. They lost their grip. Everything
started to slip, unravel, come loose
while I was standing there, and I might
be there still, if it hadn't been for

some part of me that was already
heading toward the ladder and the flight
of stairs down to the ground. Everything
got brighter as I ran, all the cracks

between the siding started to glow
and swell with light. Not a trace of wind,
no tornado screaming through the trees,
sucking on the walls, only layers

of dust and chaff that had built up all
those years working free now and spilling
through the light, leaking, spreading like smoke,
making no more sound than a whisper.

I came down the stairs through dust so thick
I couldn't see. I had almost reached
the barn door when a stray board caught me
across the neck—same place I broke it

twenty years ago, up at the lake—
and drove me straight on through the briars.
That was all that saved me: whatever
breaks is always stronger where it mends.

I don't know how long I was out. When
I came to, it was near dark, and still.
I couldn't move. Paralyzed. The barn
was down. There was nothing I could do,

nobody else knew I was out there.
It might be days, maybe even weeks,
before anybody came that far
and noticed the truck parked in the weeds.

I listened and tried to think. No birds,
that's all I could remember. Pigeons,
sparrows, nothing like that in the loft
when I first went up there. Animals

have a way of knowing. They say cows
will lie down before an earthquake hits.
I listened now. There was a cricket
somewhere in the middle of the barn,

or what used to be the barn, and now
was only a mass of lumber and scrap

no higher than a man. A cricket
first, and then a katydid, somewhere

out in the middle of all that wood.
There were lightning bugs, too, I saw them
winking on and off all around me,
but I couldn't move from where I fell.

I thought I would die then, and be like
everything else, even like the barn,
sinking back into the earth. I felt
peaceful; I could hear all the peepers

and tree frogs and night creatures singing
the way they do every summer night.
They made a sound I had always known
and not thought much about. Now I heard.

They were going to take the barn back,
everything that lived out in that woods—
'possums and squirrels and snakes and bugs.
Now that I thought about it, they were

pickers, just like I was. They came out
when no one else was around, and picked
through whatever happened to be there.
They'd take me too. It wouldn't be long.

When it got dark I could look up through
the raspberry canes and maple leaves
at the stars. They say a man's whole life
runs before him when it's time to die.

I remembered my mother coming
to get me out of bed once, waking
me up so we could go out and see
the northern lights. It was a rare sight

that far south. She held me up, pointing
into the sky. I heard her talking
to my father. They were still young then,
there was something in their voices. What

the northern lights looked like I couldn't
remember. All I could see were stars.
I liked her holding me, and him near.
I looked up at the stars now, lying

on my back, without moving, staring
straight up. They were all still there. The more
I looked the more I could see it's not
really up, at all, but out. We look

out and into. We see from a place
that floats through all that, like a lantern
carried in the dark. I knew no one
would come and find me, but I thought how

you lift the globe, and put in a match,
and the light gives off smoke, until you
turn down the wick, and adjust the flame.
Lower the globe; and now you're all set

to go out and find whatever's lost.
Starting to fall asleep in the dark
I thought I saw something glimmering
like a wick catching fire, like the light

in the barn when it started to shake.
It was daylight, morning. My father
and I were climbing up the steep roof
on our own barn to free a kite stuck

on the weathervane. We threw it down
and then went on to the end. I saw

the lightning rod up close, got to touch
the iron, all scarred and encrusted,

then bent over to look through the ball
of glass the grounding cable ran through.
For a moment I saw everything
through the blue of that ball—down below

the pasture, the creek winding through it,
the four milk cows wading in the smoke
of the willows, the sky reflecting
on the water, the water and grass

and clouds all blue, the whole world blue
as though it had always been that way
and I had never known till I got
to see it through the lightning rod's eye.

I saw it again, lying there, not
able to move—that same blue world,
full of stars now. It was the last thing
I saw before sinking into sleep.

When I woke the next day, I was still
a child, this time looking up at
my own face in a mirror: it moved,
smiled, gazed back at me. Disappeared,

so I could see trees and sky again.
Saw part of her shoulder, then her face
moving around above me, circling,
doing a little dance, looking down

but saying nothing. I tried to speak
but my lips were frozen, no words came.
Help, help, I said in my mind, go get
help, but she was farther away now

and then everything was still. Child.
Little girl. What was she doing here?
Was there anyone with her? And soon
I heard the old woman's voice coming

closer: she was picking her way through
the canes, grumbling when they stuck to her,
sometimes setting the tin buckets down
to get free, warning the child against

spilling berries they'd already picked.
Then it was her face, looking in mine
to see if I was dead or alive,
and seeing something worse than a ghost,

something that had mattered even more
to her than living or dying, once,
a long time ago—me, my own face
but thirty years later now, grown old,

gone sunken and pale, like a wax face
in a coffin. I could see her eyes
while she looked down at me, studying
what to do, even what to say now.

I'd not seen her since that first evening
I got back, in fifty-six, after
two years in Korea. Her folks had
lived out on this place; her dad farmed it.

She and I rode the same school bus;
on rainy days we played in the barn.
And when I joined the Army, she said
she would wait for me, she wrote letters

all that time, and said she was saving
herself for me, that we could get married,

but my younger brother wrote and said
she was going out with other guys.

My first night home we went out to park
in my brother's car. I took off all
her clothes and said now since you've saved it
for me I want it the way the whores

do it in Japan and she started
to cry while I took her on her knees
and made her cry even more and then
pushed her out the door and drove off

with all her clothes. I never knew how
she got home, never saw her again
after I got my discharge papers.
I heard they moved to another state.

And now here she was, it was her, make
no mistake, even with all the lines
and creases and crow's-feet—I could tell.
I could hear her breath coming hard while

she looked down at me, trying to think
what to do next, not even certain
I was still alive. I couldn't blink
or move my eyes. I think she touched me,

touched my face, my body, then my wrist,
feeling for a pulse. I'm still alive,
I tried to say, get me out of here,
I didn't mean it, I'm sorry, I'll

make it up to you somehow, after
all these years. Now she was looking straight
at me. She reached out to touch my face.
"Tears," she said, speaking for the first time.

"Tears. You bastard. Thirty years later
and you're crying." She moved back, out of
my range of vision. I heard her talk
to the little girl, who must have been

a mute. She stood over me again.
Evidently I was still crying—
tears of happiness that she would go,
come back with help, bring an ambulance,

medics, rescue team. "We're going now,"
she said simply. "It won't do to keep
fresh raspberries out in warm weather."
They moved off through the weeds, carrying

both buckets, going slow, bending back
the canes. Everything got calm again.
It was still early morning. I knew
for certain I was going to die now,

and it seemed all right this time, not much
I could do about it anyway.
I started drifting, having dreams with
nothing in them. Whether I woke up

staring into the sky, or whether
I slept till nightfall, I never knew.
Sometime in the night I entered shock;
I was unconscious the next morning.

I had no life signs when they found me
that afternoon, after I had been
lying there for almost two whole days.
Medics came in a helicopter

to lift me out of there, take me down
to a big hospital in the city.

They told me all this later, after
I spent a week in intensive care.

There's always a moment, when you first
wake up in a bright room, with nurses
wearing white dresses and little hats,
you think you've died and gone to heaven;

I wasn't dead yet, but I came close.
The man who found me came to see me
in my hospital room. He worked for
the State Police, an interpreter

of aerial photographs. They had
been studying satellite photos
of that part of the world, trying
to see where the Interstate Strangler

might have buried more of his victims.
He picked up young hitchhikers, maybe
offered them money for kinky sex,
took them to abandoned farms not far

off the interstate. They were handcuffed,
then strangled and mutilated, left
in shallow graves and covered with brush.
They had found seven graves at four sites

and they were looking for more. Sometimes
a fresh grave shows up on a photo
taken by a satellite. Sometimes
they spot a suspicious vehicle

in an unlikely place, or make out
tracks worth investigating. This man
had an old photo that showed the barn
and a brand-new one that showed the barn

changed, in some way, and my pickup parked
at the end of an untraveled lane,
on a farm they already knew was
abandoned, on their list to watch close.

They sent a team out right away with
guns drawn in case it was the Strangler
holed up there, and of course they found me
in his place. My paralysis was

only temporary. I walked out
of that hospital a week later,
a bit stiff but still able to climb
in my truck—the troopers brought it there—

and drive home. They had confiscated
the half load of barn siding but dropped
the trespassing charge. The county paid
the medevac for rescuing me,

the state picked up the tab for my stay
in the hospital. I don't know why—
maybe they added it to the cost
of catching the Strangler. They got him

a month later—by that time they knew
he drove a pickup, and this was in
all the newspapers and on TV.
A driver on the interstate saw

a hitchhiker get in a pickup
and memorized the license number
and phoned it in to the State Police
from the next rest stop. The Strangler

gave up after a high-speed chase through
three counties. They say he'll get the chair.

Me, I gave up picking barn siding.
I work strictly on old houses now,

sometimes garages. There's a demand
for copper; the price is going up.
I can rip it out of those old walls,
those basements, better than anyone.

I have to listen, pay attention,
like always. I don't want those shadows
sneaking up on me again. Sometimes
I think I died out there in the weeds

next to where that barn fell in, and I'm
a different person now, born again
but in a strange way. Sometimes I think
it was God who looked down through the lens

of that satellite camera and
saw me lying there. Sometimes I think
it was me who looked out through the eye
of the lightning rod, and saw something

that might have been God. And then there was
Retta showing up like that, as though
no time had passed, and how I asked her
to forgive me, even though I knew

she couldn't hear me. For a while
I thought she had left me there to die.
Then I understood it could have been
a lot worse. She might have had a knife

or a pair of pruning shears. No one
would have known. When they found my body,
the coroner would have chalked it up
to the Strangler. She didn't do that,

she simply went away with the girl
and the berries. It's odd to think how
even the Strangler could have passed through
a place like that, looking for something

and not finding it, then moving on.
Nobody's lived on that old farm since
the middle nineteen-fifties, nothing's
left there now but a bunch of trees set

back from the road. The other pickers
will have cleaned up the barnwood by now,
carried it off like a swarm of ants
at a picnic. One of these years when

the freeze-and-thaw works enough mortar
from between the stones, and the chimney
blows over, there won't be anything
left there except the raspberry patch.

People will still stop by—different
kinds of pickers, the ones who know where
the hickory nuts fall, out in the woods,
and where to find the best shaggymanes

and puffballs, and when it's time to look
for morels. Those people are shadows
moving along the edges, always
keeping a step ahead. Finding things

can be a calling, a way of life.
All a picker wants to do is find
something nobody else knows about,
have it for a while, then pass it on.

This story I've been telling you now,
you might say you just ran across it

by accident, but the plain truth is
we don't hear things until we're ready

and that could be a kind of finding,
too, even a way of life—paying
attention to what's happening now,
then handing it on to someone else.

You take those young men the Strangler found
standing at the side of the highway,
or waiting in one of those rest stops,
hoping for a ride to the next town:

they're no different from the rest of us,
they've come to see there's no going back,
everything is gone now, or changed from
the way it used to be. There's no shame

in what they did. They say he would talk
about helping them out, would tell them
that just past this next exit he knew
of a man who needed a good hand

to work for him for a day or two,
in this old farmhouse, fixing it up,
getting it ready to sell again.
If you hadn't eaten anything

for two or three days, or hadn't slept,
if you were flat broke and couldn't seem
to get a ride, you'd listen to him,
you'd want him to like you, be willing

to go with him while he keeps turning
down those deserted roads, those old lanes
where the signs are full of bullet holes
and the apple trees have all gone wild.

Then think of the satellite out there
in space mapping that part of the world,
looking down and seeing everything,
catching it just before it changes

but not knowing what anything is—
maybe seeing Retta and the child
walking along with their tin buckets,
maybe seeing me sliding old boards

down out of that barn loft, the Strangler
parked in the truck, talking to the boy—
while this shadow drifts out over us,
the one we can never really know.

Cicadas

Only one, and then many, scissoring
through the summer dusk, neither calling
nor answering but simply singing—
all risen from the earth, from years
of darkness inexplicable, from dust—
all having labored toward the sun
and left their nether selves behind,
their dry shells clinging—all gone
at last among the leaves, to make music
into the evening, vibration that comes
from within, that emerges, that unfolds
with wavering crescendo, and nothing—
no one, not the great cellist in the hall,
not the sound of the freight train
bearing down on you at the crossing,
no, not even the sigh of the beloved,
safe in your arms a final time,
beginning to call your name—can rise
like this, or fall away so swiftly.

Interview

Now this here rag is the one they used to call
the lost rag.

Sort of thing everybody knew and nobody ever bothered
to write down.

It was just a few licks, something you'd sit and play
by yourself,

when there was nobody else around. Maybe it was
some old man

showed you how to play it, a long time ago. You turn off
that machine,

I'm going to play it for you now. I said
turn it off.

Drawing the Antique

The Victoria and Albert ... still displays its
great collection of casts. American art museums
destroyed theirs—the Chicago Art Institute did
so, I believe, in the 1950s—or, as in the case of the
Metropolitan Museum of Art, has them in storage
in a highway viaduct. ...

Henry Hope Reed, letter to the New York Review
of Books, *17 August 1989.*

On the third floor of the old high school—
up a stairway fenced off in the late sixties
due to rising costs and squabbles over turf—
through the gate, with the principal's key,
down the barrel-vaulted hallway, along doors
nailed shut now, past rows of glass display cases
displaying nothing—
                    after turning a corner
in our explorations, we come face to face
with three life-sized plaster casts acquired
when the local art league put them up for grabs
back during the fifties.
                    Copies of copies,
on pedestals, their dim, dust-mantled features
glossy in places, luminous in the bleak light:
a Venus of some forgotten school, nipples
rubbed smooth, pudenda hammered and dented;
a wounded gladiator, fallen, overwhelmed
by marking-pencil swastikas; a statesman,
uplifted hand corroded, structural wires
bleeding through.
                    They wait here, faces battered,
noses chipped away, lips stained yellow where

countless cigarette butts, moistened with spit,
were carefully stuck.
                    Left in this dark place
they become more like their lost originals,
true to some ideal we can barely imagine now.
Yet we are shocked, we know them instantly—
recognizable as victims everywhere, shapes
destroyed and timeless,
                    still able to instruct.

For an Old Flame

When the news came, there was nothing left,
none of those old trappings. When you spoke,
no sound emerged. I knew it was neither dream
nor vision—those categories had broken down,
nothing remained. You stood somewhere
in a junkyard—surrounded by piles
of rusted and broken bodies, doors gone,
engines disemboweled, windows shattered—
where they had brought your compact car
after the head-on collision. Here
you had come too, inevitably, since
the dead have no other place to go
in this world we have made: nothing waits
beyond, no light escapes from the horizon
of physical events. Occasionally
a couple of teenaged boys wander by,
with vise grips and adjustable wrenches,
looking for cheap parts for their dragster.
Here you could stay forever, unnoticed
among the mountains of rust and old rubber,
the soiled back seats, the glove compartments
with their forgotten artifacts. It remains
only for me to set you now in the prow
of an all-black '57 Chevrolet hardtop
with dual carburetors and glass-packed
mufflers, and pay the ferryman the coins
from your eyes, and see you start out,
not looking back, over those dark waters.

Portrait Studio

Still here, then, the antique letters in gold,
the sun-bleached faces peering through the glass;
all of them still waiting. The old backdrops
have stayed the same, the hand-painted curtains,
you do not have to look twice to see them
standing before those frozen waterfalls,
those cedar boughs, those far peaks capped with snow.
Instead, you climb the staircase wedged between
the dime store and the drugstore, you go up
into the hallway, the gray corridor,
you find the right words on the frosted pane.
Step in, and the photographer appears,
drying his hands on his apron, just popped
out of the darkroom, no helper today.
In the studio everything is piled
and pushed to the back; it was his father's
before he took it over. The windows
are boarded up with what used to be called
"car siding"—varnished once, but peeling now.
You spin the wooden stool, and sit down.
While he moves the spotlights and reflectors,
while he fusses with the camera angle,
while he asks about your daughter, your eyes
begin to see shapes beyond the brightness,
and you sense that in the finished portrait
he will show you gazing out of shadows
your father knew, even your grandfather.
There will be a patch of light hovering
in the background, just above your shoulders,
and beyond that, toward the edge, a darkness.
Part of what appears there will be painted,
part will be reflection, and part will be
something into which you have been growing
all this time—as though an old cloak, made up
of many folds and gathers, still being
held out for you, almost fitted you now.

Cecropia Moth

It was only you, come out of the willows, drying your wings
for the first time in something you had never known before—
not the slow glimmer of silk your ghost had wrapped around you,
not the wind's rustle in the branches, but light: I saw it too,

I stood in the same stillness, just after daybreak, thinning
and cutting back the canes of the rose bush in the side yard,
and I noticed your shadow at first—something pulsing there
among the leaves—then looked again, and saw it was you,

that you were waiting for a moment neither of us could tell,
that would only come as the sun rose higher. So I went on
with my work, my pruning and severing, and you continued
with yours, there in the shade, in the half-light of morning.

After I had made a pile of dead canes, I returned to the place
where you have been resting, and looked through the branches,
and saw you were gone. Sometimes I have noticed the shadow
of a hawk's wings on the grass, but looked around too late—

or turned the wrong way—and seen nothing. Nor am I certain,
even now, what came over us. Yet I know it was there—perhaps
when I put a match to the canes, and watched them give off fire,
sudden and fierce, and black smoke, too, all rising together.

Seed Storm

Now I know, watching their slow falling,
that the cottonwoods are not simply speaking
but have begun to sing, in their own way,

and that the feathery notes sifting down
all around us on this late May afternoon
are only a dream of snowfall, of weather

we have come through, all of us, everything
that moves or breathes or waves in the wind.
Ahead of us now the whiteness descending

gathers in drifts in the grass and flows
down the pathways, catching at peonies bent
with heaviness, poppies starting to scatter—

and I understand, as though these gestures
were the language of some ancient chorus,
that I have entered my fiftieth summer

walking beneath these trees, all of them
members of the poplar family, whose leaves
still quiver, even when there is no wind.

Look, the air is so calm now the seed storm
no longer seems to fall, while we ourselves
are what is rising, up into that trembling.

Galleynipper

Where we might go, in the summers, to a cabin on the big lake
and spend time there in the light, my sister and I, doing
nothing, playing in the sand, slowly turning brown and learning
to see through the glare, my mother with her book, her sunbonnet,

and nights in that room of open rafters, curtains drawn against
a cold wind off the bay. If we were good, she would let us have
one candle, in a saucer on the deal table, in the exact center
of our bedroom, that we could not touch, but only watch making

shadows among the iron headboards, the rafters, the curved frame
of the mirror: until we saw our own faces, in a strange slow dusk,
swimming out past a point where we would be taken by the waves
and carried under, into a darkness that beat nightlong outside

our window. Not once did I outlast the candle's glimmering,
to know true blackness, but lay there watching through a blur
of lashes, through my own weariness, hearing my sister begin
her even rowing toward that other shore, waiting to see what

insect or flying creature chance might allow in the room
through a crack in the door or a tear in the screen. Watched
how they preened themselves in the light, how they tilted
toward its center: moth the color of sand, midge or miller hatched

out of dust, and about to return, rendered mad now, taking
leave of their senses, erratically orbiting, coming in closer,
changing the shadows too, casting up their own ghosts, adding
to the slow beating carrying me toward sleep—shapes that would be

only a pool of wax and grit by morning, smudge of wick, drift
of gauzy wing caught like amber. But one of these creatures
alone came as though summoned not by flame but by light itself,
content to float back and forth above the beds, the sleeping

sister, and long ago I heard my mother call it by its old
Hoosier name, this pale, slow-moving, slow-beating, hushed fly
or harmless mosquito that seemed undrawn by fire, and hovered
beneath the rafters, or skimmed the walls, as though searching—

galleynipper, she called it, that comes at the wind's rising,
that asks nothing, that is huge and slow and going nowhere
except back and forth in the shadows, that will not hurt you,
that is too wise to believe in a candle or its dark image

guttering, past midnight, in a patched and scaling mirror.
Galleynipper, that had come for me, that would carry me high
above the waves, the sleeping figures adrift, even above
the light, and I would know when we had come to the right place.

Changeling

Such, men do changelings call, so changed by faery's theft.
Spenser

Even now I remember them slipping over the sill—
curtains blowing, a light softened by new leaves
and scattering across the ceiling—and I could see
the room in the dresser mirror, from where I lay
in my crib, and know, long before I had guessed
at speech, or where it might take me, that creatures
casting no reflection had come to steal me away.

And only emerged from that trance as a man, grown,
out boating with a friend on a clear river flowing
through a green world, looking down into the water
grazed by our shadow, sensing what passed below—
and hearing him tell how the hunter scans ahead
and beyond the trees, knows in advance what deer
will do, stays in one place until they step forward.

So when my mother went out to the garden, singing
in the light, they were hiding beneath my window,
waiting to take me, and leave another, who was also me,
but changed—as old and fixed in the ways of song
as the hunter who watches, the water that slips by
unceasingly, and is always clear, never the same.
How can I reach those stories now, I who make

no ripple on the stream's surface, and drift instead
toward some wide and lasting place where the water
merges with the sky and the land? Each night I wait
to be changed again, to hear her singing, to know
they have only borrowed me, and are bringing me back,
having taught me to see, through shadow, where each deer
walks in the meadow, and which will be left, which taken.

74

Mourning Doves

That all my life I have listened to the calls
of mourning doves, have heard them hidden far back
under the eaves, or perched among sycamore branches—
their five still notes sometimes lost in the wind—
and not known how to answer: this I confess,
lying here now, on a summer morning, in a dark room
no less lit by the sound of their soft calling

than by your breathing. And though you might dream
that I lie stretched beside you, I am alone again,
and a child, hearing these same dim voices drifting
high outside my window, explaining to myself how
these are the cries of the newly dead, in the dawn light,
rising toward heaven. Only that, and a child's need
to make up stories on falling asleep, or waking.

And though you might speak, out of that dream, or form
some forbidden word on your lips, my response
would be no more than the music two of them can make—
matching their notes in time, setting up harmonies
that are clear, and pure, and accidental even
to their own reckoning, since all of their singing
is circular, and comes back to the same stillness.

It is back to that place they are calling us now,
and it is out of not knowing that I brush away
strands of hair from your face, and begin to kiss
your eyes, your lips—that I might take sleep
from your mouth into mine, that we might dream invention,
and you hear my confession, and I your answering,
like a song traded back and forth in the morning light.

The Believers

Shakertown at Pleasant Hill, Kentucky, at the winter solstice.

These are the old dreads whispering to me
through the slant light of the meeting hall
this wintry afternoon. Mother Ann Lee
is here, raising a splintery hand to call
for lines to form between the facing walls
and dance the figures that can bring to pass
a momentary clearing of the darkened glass.

A blaze of dying sun brings out the grain
across the wooden floor. Outside this space
their bodies could not touch, nor long remain
together, else some elder's wrinkled face
shone down, from its high watching place,
and shamed them. Here, desire slipped its rein,
the better to be harnessed on a higher plane.

To save by giving what one cannot keep—
mortal to dance, and by such whirling come
into immortal worlds—while others sleep,
to waken from the body's dark mysterium—
these were the steps she taught. And once begun,
there was no turning back, no way to slake
this thirst for otherness except to shake.

And as a tree in winter fills with crows
convened out of some harsh necessity
till every branch is bent and overflows
into a mirroring of what one sees
in summer—creatures become leaves,
all turning, turning in a dark repose—
so did they circle here, and come in close

until they flowered, and it was summer now,
by Shawnee Run, near the stone landing,
where fireflies had filled a sycamore
with single light, and all who saw, standing
along the shore, knew a sure commanding
in that pulse, and walked there, bright
and dark by turns, in the summer night.

None of that charmed singing in the air
above their heads has lasted, nothing remains
of what it meant to dance the hollow square,
to walk the narrow path, the endless chain.
Not even the sun's slow march explains—
here, they kept time simply by the swing
of a lead bullet fastened to a string.

The guided tour moves on. I cross the floor
through triangles of light and shade, done
with imagining, yet pausing at the door
to look back on this room, and how the sun
reveals, for just a moment, what will come
when we are finally shaken, and by grace,
no longer darkly see, but face to face.

For Starr Atkinson, Who Designed Books

Oldest of words, of sounds: star.
Everything of that name perishes.
The sun will reclaim each planet,
the galaxy collapse, light itself
siphon down into a last darkness.

From you I learned how images balance
in the white space of each page,
how pages unfold like leaves,
how light and dark interpenetrate,
how what we do will not be noticed.

Light from those stars coming deep
from space, reaching our own eyes
in darkness, at the top of a hill;
words on a page keeping the old sounds,
the ones worth saying another time.

From *Les Barricades Mystérieuses* | 1999

Improvisation

To improvise, first let your fingers stray
across the keys like travelers in snow:
each time you start, expect to lose your way.

You'll find no staff to lean on, none to play
among the drifts the wind has left in rows.
To improvise, first let your fingers stray

beyond the path. Give up the need to say
which way is right, or what the dark stones show;
each time you start, expect to lose your way.

And what the stillness keeps, do not betray;
the one who listens is the one who knows.
To improvise, first let your fingers stray;

out over emptiness is where things weigh
the least. Go there, believe a current flows
each time you start: expect to lose your way.

Risk is the pilgrimage that cannot stay;
the keys grow silent in their smooth repose.
To improvise, first let your fingers stray.
Each time you start, expect to lose your way.

Summons

A log shifts, sending a few sparks higher.
Outside, through the larches, an owl calls.
The dog's asleep. On the hearth near the fire,

carefully stacked, in a basket of woven wire,
wood for the night. A stick of kindling falls,
a log shifts, sending a few sparks higher,

changing the shadows in the room. A spire
of light glints on the clock's face in the hall.
The dog's asleep. On the hearth, near the fire,

he begins to whine, to become a far crier
among the hills, twitching his feathered paws.
A log shifts, sending a few sparks higher;

his ears prick: ahead, some stark desire
steps forth, waiting to hold him in thrall.
The dog's asleep on the hearth, near the fire;

he is farther away now, part of a choir
of lost voices. He falls back, sprawls.
A log shifts, sending a few sparks higher;
the dog's asleep on the hearth near the fire.

Candle

It is your naked body now I see,
released from all restraint, once more revealed
among the shadows, where you wait to be.

What incorporeal fire, what lambency
could be as bright? Brilliant and unconcealed,
it is your naked body now I see

where facing mirrors gleam. That transiency—
the deepening of your image there—will yield,
among the shadows, where you wait to be,

a nether self—a rising on the sea,
a wind that moves across an open field.
It is your naked body now I see

approaching, yet projected endlessly
away from me, by some enchantment sealed
among the shadows. Where you wait to be,

the parallels converge, the mystery
remains: what comes together is the real.
It is your naked body now I see
among the shadows, where you wait to be.

Berceuse

Step down into that darkness now, that dream
of drifting unremembrance and release,
where words and music form an endless stream

of syllables that swirl away and gleam
upon the flow, then vanish without cease.
Step down into that darkness: now that dream—

that fragment wave which in one moment seems
to break—returns, and on the next increase,
where words and music form an endless stream,

floods all resistance, all that would deem
mere waking marvelous, or knowledge peace.
Step down; into that darkness now, that dream,

descend, not to renounce but to redeem
the surface world. Within the water's lease,
where words and music form an endless stream,

letters appear in lines that have no theme
or purpose, yet their passing brings surcease.
Step down into that darkness now, that dream
where words and music form an endless stream.

Ditchweed

In the forgotten places where it still grows,
they come with green trash bags and gunnysacks.
No one every sees anything, no one knows

what happens here. They walk down endless rows
of soybeans, out along the railroad tracks,
in the forgotten places. Where it still grows,

the banks own everything now. From windows
in the old farmhouses, no one glances back,
no one ever sees anything. No one knows

who drew the penciled map, or if it shows
the right way. Near woodpiles and hayracks,
in the forgotten places where it still grows,

wagons rust in the tall grass. Nobody mows
the weeds along those roads, or tars the cracks.
No one ever sees anything, no one knows

whose car is parked beside the bridge. SLOW
is the only sign the hunters leave intact
in the forgotten places. Where it still grows,
no one ever sees anything, no one knows.

Cemetery

Broken tombstones, paper flags—one sways,
held by a thread. Wind in the cedar trees.
Two blacksnakes come together in the maze

of shifting light—a momentary haze
of darkness shows among the jimson weeds,
broken tombstones, paper flags. One sways,

rests on a ledge, holding a level gaze;
the other waits—poised—tasting the breeze.
Two blacksnakes come together. In the maze

of sun and shadow, shot with beveled rays,
they drift among the green interstices,
broken tombstones, paper flags. One sways,

the other flows around it, sending waves
of permutation through the random leaves.
Two blacksnakes come together. In the maze

behind them, down the narrow passageways,
the grass unbends, the dimpled spider weaves.
Broken tombstones, paper flags—one sways.
Two blacksnakes come together in the maze.

Interlude

Here is the spring I promised we would find
if we came back this way—a hollow space
beneath the hillside, waiting all this time

for us to angle through the leaves, and climb
down to the ledge, to where it slows its pace.
Here is the spring I promised we would find,

with elderberry blossoming, and thyme
and saxifrage along the limestone face.
Beneath the hillside, waiting all this time,

the falls, in overflowing steps, combine
to form an unexpected stopping-place.
Here is the spring I promised we would find:

across the pool, the accidental lines
and endless circles merge—a constant grace
beneath the hillside, waiting. All this time

has brought us here—to listen to the pines,
to drink, to watch the water-striders race.
Here is the spring I promised we would find
beneath the hillside, waiting all this time.

Ford

A place of crossing over, where the river
starts its turn—a drift of glacial rocks
reveals a path, within the current's shadow,

to the other side. Here, streams of minnows
slip through the shallows, as if to mark
a place of crossing. Over where the river

broods, near the far bank, a fallen cedar,
bleached and smooth, stripped of its bark,
reveals a path. Within the current's shadow,

up close, the rocks have no special order;
you must choose, with each step you take,
a place of crossing over. Where the river

tangles and snarls but fails to scatter
the stones—that fracture, that break,
reveals a path within. The current's shadow

overwhelms you, there's no sign to follow,
no pattern now—your own momentum makes
a place of crossing over, where the river
reveals a path within the current's shadow.

Millefiori

In the last glimmer of late afternoon,
burnished by the sun's oblique farewell,
a mirror shines, across an empty room,

a shimmering patch of light. A subtle fume
of brightness creeps along the dusty shelves
in the last glimmer of late afternoon;

immersed in shadow, rows of books are strewn
with dazzling motes. Like circles in a well,
a mirror shines across an empty room,

reaching from pen to letter knife, to spoon
and cup—as though reflection might dispel,
in the last glimmer of late afternoon,

oncoming night. Unhurried, like the moon's
ascent, or honey tipped from gleaming cells,
a mirror shines across an empty room,

a paperweight of myriad flowers blooms,
a softness flares within a whorled shell.
In the last glimmer of late afternoon
a mirror shines across an empty room.

Clavichord

Touch me once more, until these separate strands
begin to stir. My inarticulate keys
quicken beneath your soft, attentive hands,

my strings, responsive to your least commands,
give back strange overtones and harmonies.
Touch me once more. Until these separate strands

comply, and nothing hurried countermands
the way in which such gradual urgencies
quicken beneath your soft, attentive hands,

there can be no release—nor sarabandes
of meaning—in these plangent melodies.
Touch me once more, until these separate strands

commingle, and a newfound world expands
between us in this little room. Let seas
quicken beneath your soft, attentive hands,

let continents appear: who understands
this music loosens vast geographies.
Touch me once more, until these separate strands
quicken beneath your soft, attentive hands.

Tankroom

Come together at last, no longer strangers,
braceleted with numbers, stripped of names,
asleep and drifting in these still waters,

they share a timeless urge—to be forever
lost in each other's arms, having no shame,
come together at last. No longer strangers,

they touch in casual ways we half remember—
moored in the twilight, tethered by a chain,
asleep and drifting. In these still waters

they dream of the moment when their fetters
will be struck off. Released from all blame,
come together at last, no longer strangers,

they will find their way. Now they encounter
only darkness enfolding, and endless rain.
Asleep and drifting in these still waters,

they must be born again, as broken embers
carried on the wind, or fragments of flame
come together at last—no longer strangers
asleep and drifting in these still waters.

Phosphorescence

What passed between us once was but a dream
that cast no shadow on the world of things.
Think of me now, in these dark days, as flame

that in a scattering of cubes still seems
to rise up from the vanished tree's lost rings.
What passed between us once was but a dream,

a slow and inverse fire that fell like rain
and shook the ashes from its brooding wings.
Think of me now, in these dark days, as flame

that burns in some unearthly way, like green
and silver branches dense with blossoming.
What passed between us once was but a dream,

a glimpse of loosened raiment, partially seen,
that falls away, and yet in falling, clings.
Think of me now, in these dark days, as flame

that with a colder, lasting light redeems
whatever loss such bright remembrance brings.
What passed between us once was but a dream.
Think of me now, in these dark days, as flame.

Palimpsest

The walk that led out through the apple trees—
the narrow, crumbling path of brick embossed
among the clumps of grass, the scattered leaves—

has vanished now. Each spring the peonies
come back, to drape their heavy bolls across
the walk that led out through the apple trees,

as if to show the way—until the breeze
dismantles them, and petals drift and toss
among the clumps of grass. The scattered leaves

half fill a plaited basket left to freeze
and thaw, and gradually darken into moss.
The walk that led out through the apple trees

has disappeared—unless, down on your knees,
searching beneath the vines that twist and cross
among the clumps of grass, the scattered leaves,

you scrape, and find—simplest of mysteries,
forgotten all this time, but not quite lost—
the walk that led out through the apple trees
among the clumps of grass, the scattered leaves.

Labyrinth

Somewhere, within the murmuring of things
that make no difference—aimlessly playing,
drifting in the wind—a loose door swings,

banging against a wall; the piece of string
that held it shut has blown away. Delaying,
somewhere within the murmuring of things,

crickets and tree toads pause, listening;
now they go on with their shrill surveying.
Drifting in the wind, a loose door swings

in widening arcs. Each rusty iron hinge
creaks in a different key: each is decaying,
somewhere within. The murmuring of things

wells up—the quickening thrum of wings,
the pulsing, intersecting voices swaying,
drifting in the wind. A loose door swings;

no torch, no adventitious thread brings
meaning to this maze, this endless straying
somewhere within the murmuring of things.
Drifting in the wind, a loose door swings.

Linen

Scattered among bundles of flax in the rain,
pinned under water by smooth stones—broken,
spun, wound, and gathered in bright skeins

of blond thread, like bronze or silk—I gained
knowledge of the old ways long unspoken,
scattered among bundles of flax. In the rain

I was scutched to the marrow, yet no pain
could reach me—I had become that token
spun, wound, and gathered. In bright skeins

of filament, to be woven—to be changed
into pattern, as though having woken,
scattered among bundles of flax in the rain,

but risen up through darkness, newly arrayed
with morning. And would become, in time, omen
spun, wound, and gathered in bright skeins

of light, rags into paper, unconstrained
words cast there like silk, or bronze gnomon—
scattered among bundles of flax in the rain,
spun, wound, and gathered in bright skeins.

Reprise

Only an evening wind that comes at last
before sleep falls—a distant beckoning
so long forgotten, out of dark rains past—

wind that the scent of water lilies, massed
and set adrift and softly gleaming, brings.
Only an evening wind, that comes at last

and carries memory with it, anchored fast
in the flow of things. Hushed imaginings,
so long forgotten, out of dark rains past,

or hands that rest now, in the aftermath
of music echoing deep within the strings.
Only an evening wind, that comes at last,

that has no shape or form, nor earthly task
except to draw up from those hidden springs
so long forgotten, out of dark rains past,

an elemental motion. Hearing, we ask,
and yet we know, beyond all reckoning—
only an evening wind that comes at last,
so long forgotten, out of dark rains past.

Hawkmoth

Freed of all cerements of sleep, unfurled
in shadow—touch me now with your wings'
imagined light, lift me toward your world

of vision, of dark flight. When I would curl
inchoate, show me these luminescent things
freed of all cerements of sleep. Unfurled,

I searched the labyrinth, but night hurled
me into nothingness; teach me to sing,
imagined light, lift me. Toward your world

tempt me along the winding path, whirled
by its dust, its storms, that I might spring—
freed of all cerements of sleep—unfurled

upon the naked day, and by some structural
fury or design, from out of darkness bring
imagined light. Lift me toward your world,

riddler, through all the chaos and the swirl,
find me out deeply with your soft sting,
freed of all cerements of sleep, unfurled.
Imagined light, lift me toward your world.

Comet

Somewhere not far beyond these barricades
mysterious, a single branch is burning.
To the dim light and the large circle of shade

I would return, and by green leaves arrayed
with broken fire, regain a different learning,
somewhere not far beyond. These barricades

are all instruction now, these sounds evade
the measure, and the swarm's impulsive churning.
To the dim light and the large circle of shade

I would be summoned—image shattered, made
again into a thousand shapes of yearning,
somewhere not far. Beyond these barricades

the scattered pieces come together, swayed
by spectral lines that draw the most discerning
to the dim light and the large circle of shade.

Along this path we cannot be conveyed
but move as particles or waves, returning—
somewhere not far, beyond these barricades—
to the dim light and the large circle of shade.

From Cross *This Bridge* at a *Walk* | 2006

Covered Bridge

At a family reunion in 1983, Baxter Decker, the author's maternal uncle, who was born in 1909, agrees to speak—into a cassette recorder—his recollections of a story told to him by his great-grandfather, George Barnabas Decker. It is a tale of a chance encounter in the summer of 1863 during the War between the States.

1. WHAT BAXTER WAS TOLD.

When you come up to the river at floodtide
on a bright summer's day with wind churning
the trees and the marsh water riffling silver
among the cattails and no other way across

except the bridge—where it was darkness
on first entering, until your eyes adjusted,
with the gleaming square at the other end,
your horse skittish on the echoing boards—

the thin light coming through cracks, from
all directions, even beneath where you stand
and you can peer down through warped planks
and see water moving—that dizzy sideways

streaming—and at the same time feel wind
slipping through the length of the shaft
strong enough to blow the hat off your head—
then the sense comes to you (even the horse

understands, trembling) that the bridge
itself is moving, in long, slow rhythms
like some sort of creaking weathervane
or needle balanced over fields of force—

so when three mounted rebel soldiers stop
at the east-bank entrance, they look inside

and see my great-grandfather with the last
of twenty armloads of brush he has piled

against the center arch so that the draft
will fan the embers straight up to the roof
and fire the cedar shakes. The whole bridge
will last about as long as a pine torch

on election day. He glances up from his work
and sees the rebs reined in, watching. Three
against one, but he knows their saddlebags
are weighted down with slabs of jowl bacon

and coffee-grinders and bolts of calico
and God knows what other kinds of plunder
taken these last ten days. If it comes to a race
he can probably outrun them, even on Old Fly—

who is tethered at the west end, switching
his tail, occasionally nudging gravel loose
from the roadbed—part of the steady stream
of sand and grit and pebbles sifting down

into the waters far below. Starting out
that morning my great-grandfather had stuck
a ball pistol in his belt—the same one
he carried when he rode off to Mexico

with Lew Wallace and the First Indiana.
Never fired a shot in that campaign, never
even made it to Buena Vista. Now, it was
too much trouble to load the damned thing.

The rebs are still watching. Rather than
venture onto the bridge, they turn away
from the entrance. "Be a shame to burn such
a fine-lookin' bridge," one of them calls.

Fly shifts around nervously and knocks loose
more pebbles. Except for a tendency to bite
now and then, he was a good horse, not the least
handicapped by being ten years old and owned

by a carpenter and schoolteacher—callings
my great-grandfather followed, when he wasn't
out burning bridges, or trying to save the Union
and the State of Indiana from sure perdition

now that Morgan's raiders had been loosed on
northern soil. My great-grandfather, Barnabas,
has eight sulfur matches in his coat pocket.
He has already spied the bolt on one of the beams

where he intends to strike them, one after
the other, in a wind that continues to howl
the length of the bridge—hoping that he can
cup his fingers around at least one match

and get the conflagration started. Now
the captain (as it turns out) has dismounted
and is walking this way, the new vibrations
spooking Old Fly until my great-grandfather

calls to him, tells him to stop that whining.
He draws the pistol and lays it on a side brace.
The captain comes on, slowly, up to where
all the brush is stacked. He wears a uniform

so smudged you can't tell what army he's in.
His eyes are bloodshot; he hasn't shaved or
slept in five days. Two bars and a plated sword.
Touches his hat. "Sir, would you happen to be

a gambling man?" George Barnabas Decker nods.
The captain smiles. "That's good to know.

My men back there had a mind to ride in here
and shoot you. Fortunately, I dissuaded them.

It has always been my concern that politics
not come before good manners. We have been
out for a look at your state, and I must say
it is exceptionally handsome. But to business:

You have my personal word that General Morgan
has no intention of riding in this direction.
I am equally confident that you are under orders
to let nothing stop you from burning this bridge.

Therefore"—and as though plucked from the air,
a deck of cards appeared in his right hand—
"I propose we cut for high card. You win,
I and my troopers withdraw, so that you may

continue to carry out your orders. I win,
and you cease and desist." At this, Old Fly
lingeringly broke wind. The captain grinned.
"I was about to say we'd take your horse, too,

but now that he has come out so strongly
for Union, I am not sure he could be trusted.
You may keep your horse, sir. But if you lose,
you will withdraw, giving us your word of honor

that this bridge will not be harmed, insofar
as it is in your power to protect it. You may
tell your commander that you were driven off
by a superior force, against considerable odds."

2. WHAT BARNABAS SAID.

"Now, I helped build that bridge, as a young man,"
Barnabas told me, many years later, "working

for Old Man Hogsett, who spit tobacco juice
on the bolts, for grease, while we tightened

them up. Spent two long, blistering months
on a crew of six, fitting those big timbers,
wading up to my ass in all that mud, getting
kicked and bit by those damned bluenose mules

and all the time that old man cussing me out,
slobbering brown spit everywhere, and swearing
I'd never be a carpenter's apprentice in hell.
I tell you I was damned unhappy to see that reb

bring out that deck of cards. That morning,
when the mayor told me to get down there,
I was looking forward to burning that bridge.
To make matters worse, as a young roustabout

I had played faro and low ball and blackjack
up and down both sides of the Ohio River
as far south as Cairo, and I knew a tin-plated
smooth-talking Kentucky card-shark the minute

he opened his mouth. Had a better chance
of cutting that bridge loose and floating it
downriver and giving it to Jeff Davis himself
than I did drawing high card against that

back-room bushwhacker from Bowling Green.
'Surely you'll allow me to cut the cards?'
I said in my best riverboat gambler's voice.
The captain leaned over and laid the deck

on one of those twelve-inch, hand-dressed beams,
alongside that damned empty pistol. Right away
the wind whipped the first two or three cards
off the deck and blew them on down the bridge

but the captain never turned a hair. I saw
that tucked in his sash he had a horse pistol
with a bore as big as one of those bridge bolts;
it occurred to me he did not go about with

this piece unloaded. More cards kept blowing
away and he just stood there, waiting for me
to move. I reached out and stopped the cards
from blowing, then cut them with one hand.

He nodded and smiled, and I took off the six
of diamonds. He started to take a card, but
at that moment the other two rebs rode up,
their stolen appaloosas moving like smoke.

They'd been out reconnoitering the east bank;
now they dismounted at the entrance. Suddenly
a gust of wind lifted the deck into the air.
'I'll get them cards for you, Sir!' the boy

called out, but the captain raised a hand.
'That was our last deck,' he said, watching
the cards flutter away. He turned to me:
'How many matches have you got?' 'Only eight,'

I said. 'That's all I could find this morning.'
'Well then,' he said, 'it's settled. It's
the bridge against Fate, in a howling gale.
Each of us has two tries to light the pile.'

They commenced to bet among themselves,
rummaging through their pockets, finding
jack-knives and cameo rings and ivory combs.
The boy even had a horned toad in a cigar box

but they made him throw it away, nudge it
through a broken place in the bridge floor.

'It will be perfectly all right down there,'
the captain assured him. Finally they were ready.

The captain and the boy bet against the bridge,
the older man for it. The captain asked me
for the matches. He gave back two, passed
four out to the men, kept the last two himself.

The boy gave a rebel yell and got down
and scrunched up a handful of dead leaves
and after a bad start managed to get it going
with the second match, even making some smoke

before the wind blew it out. The older man,
who looked like he wanted do it the easy way
and shoot me on the spot—he simply struck
both matches and tossed them toward the pile.

The captain frowned. Now it was my turn.
I opened my coat against the wind and snapped
the match with my thumbnail, and got it
going good, then knelt, still holding it,

and reached it over to the pile; in the next
instant the wind snuffed it out. One down.
Stepping forward, the captain produced a bill
from his waistcoat, and held it up: bank note

recently stolen and already worthless, from
the looks of it. He wadded it up, struck a match
and got it going, then tossed it onto the brush
where it began to uncurl, burning all the while.

Old Fly, made nervous by the strange horses
tied at the east end of the bridge, chose
this particular moment to rear and whinny,
and the rebel mounts began to stamp and neigh.

One of the ponies skittered onto the bridge;
twigs from the pile fell through the cracks,
scattering onto the river below. The captain
and I each had one match left. The wind

was at gale force now, we could hear it
whipping through the trees on both sides
of the river, and rattling the loose shingles.
He knelt, in his spurred boots and greatcoat,

using his hat to shield the flame that sprang
from his last match. 'Hit's a-goin' t' go!'
the boy called, and we all leaned down but
the leaves were too green, the wind too strong;

wisps of smoke curled and blew away. 'Well, sir,'
the captain said, turning to me. 'Your turn.
You have the last match, I believe.' I did,
and when I held it up thunder and lightning

broke simultaneously in the sky above our heads
as though I had drawn them down—the storm
the mayor had warned me about finally arrived,
sheets of rain suddenly lashing at the roof

and walls of the bridge, the horses like to
jumping out of their skins the way everything
began swaying back and forth. "We better be
gettin' off this here bridge!" the older man

shouted, but the captain, as if hypnotized
by that last match, stood firm: the light
in his eyes was that of a man who has stayed—
seen and raised every bet on the table,

and then called, earned the right to see
what you've got in the hole. 'Mighty handsome

bridge,' he said, scratching his nose but still
keeping his eye on me and that matchstick.

'Nothing comparable down where we come from.'
'That's for damn sure,' the older man said.
The boy said nothing. They all looked at me.
Fly looked like he was about ready to sneeze.

Summer storms are peculiar—the way a wind
as strong as a cyclone can blow one minute
and then get still the next. The rain stopped
all of a sudden, and we could hear the horses

whickering, sand sifting through the cracks,
the sound of water whirling below us. I struck
the match. It burned steady as a wax candle
on Easter morning. It even made light there

in all those shadows. The captain took off
his hat. The two scouts stood beside him.
'Go ahead,' he said. I turned with the match
and put it to the nest of leaves, where flames

fairly leapt up into the brush, crackling and
snapping. The boy and the older man whooped
and hollered and took off for their horses.
This spooked Fly, who reared and broke loose

and came thundering through the bridge past
the place where we stood, as though he were
hell bent on having a bite of rebel horseflesh.
The captain and I ran, too, clear to the east fork,

where we could look back and see the fire
rising and spreading and going good now.
The boy caught up with Fly and gentled him
and brought him over to me. We mounted up.

Once I was in the saddle I was confounded
when the captain reached out and handed me
the ball pistol I had plumb forgot and left
back there to burn up in the flames. I told you

he was a sly one; I knew that, the minute
I laid eyes on him. After the older man
had paid up what he lost, the scouts galloped
ahead, on out of sight. We rode for a piece

in the drizzle of rain. It was letting up.
We could look back and see clouds of smoke
boiling from the center of the bridge. Flames
broke out here and there among the shakes.

'Well,' the captain said, 'I'm much obliged.
I'll trade this old buck knife back to him
before we reach the Ohio line. But I'm still ahead
by half a slab of bacon, and this turnip watch.

And you, sir, far from having diverted
General Morgan and his notorious raiders,
have set fire to a bridge that half the county
depended on to get their goods to market.'

I nodded but said nothing. 'I must say,'
he went on, 'you're a likeable fellow.
And a gambler to boot. I'm truly sorry
I can't take you prisoner. No point in that,

however, since we'll all be prisoners
before this is over. That, or corpses,
moldering in our graves.' He smiled
to himself, as though recognizing where

that last phrase had come from. 'So far,
we haven't had much luck at persuading

any of you Hoosiers to go along with us.'
'No,' I told him, 'but it would look better

if I had to walk back home.' 'Precisely,'
he said. 'As though you had struggled
against a superior force, and succeeded,
firing the bridge despite considerable odds.'

He glanced at Fly. 'That's not much of a horse.
Don't look like conscript material to me.
What's his name?' 'Fly. Old Fly.' 'Had him
long?' 'Seven years,' I said. 'He minds.'

'We'll take him along for a few miles,' he said.
'Won't be the war's first escaped prisoner.
He'll probably be home along about sundown.'
Behind us, the bridge crossbeams were yellow

with fire. The sky was beginning to clear.
We reached a bend in the road, and stopped.
The captain sat on his horse, looking back
at the burning bridge. 'War,' he said.

'A tragic and senseless affair. I've found
there's no way to get through such stupidity
unless a man can make a wager now and then
on something that don't matter anyhow,

one way or the other. I'll tell you what.
I'll bet you a quarter-eagle gold piece
that Old Fly here beats you home.' We both
laughed. At that instant Fly stretched over

and tried to bite his horse. I drew him in,
and got him settled down, then slipped
out of the saddle and handed the reins up
to the captain. To my surprise he leaned down

suddenly, the way a born cavalryman can do,
and embraced me, as though we were old friends
saying goodbye, parting for the last time.
He straightened up, touched the brim of his hat,

and rode off briskly, drawing Fly behind him.
When I got back to town the mayor came out
to meet me, wearing his Mexican War uniform.
Fly had turned up half an hour earlier,

and they were starting to get worried. I had
fired the bridge, like they said, and wanted
only to go home. Next day they claimed I was
a hero, and deserved a medal, but I laughed

and told them they'd sing a different tune
when it came time to drive the hogs. Besides,
details from Gettysburg were coming in,
and they had other things to think about."

3. GOING FISHING.

It wasn't until seven years later, when Grant
was in the White House, that Schuyler Colfax—
whose sister lived in Mississinewa County—
shook loose the money to build a new bridge.

It was a trestle bridge made of iron girders,
a quarter mile upstream from the point
where the old bridge stood. Barnabas Decker,
who watched it being built, and made sure

they did it right, lived on until 1920,
and died in his ninetieth year. Summer days
during the First War he used to take me fishing
off that iron bridge, and he would point out

the two limestone piers—the middle one gone—
where the covered bridge once stood. He would
help me bait my hook, and show me how to cast
my line out toward the most promising pools.

We would lean on the struts, keeping an eye
on our bobbers, and he would tell the story
of how he fired the first bridge, and saved
the town of Somerset from sure destruction

at the hands of the rebel invasionary force.
And if I didn't catch anything, sometimes
he would take out the thick leather wallet
he carried, and sort through all the bills

and clippings and membership cards in lodges
that hadn't held a meeting in twenty years,
and find, somewhere in that mass of papers,
wrapped squarely in what he called "a piece

of foolscap"—would actually let me hold
in my hand a creased, worn playing card,
so dim and faded it might have been a six
of diamonds, once upon a time, but now

looked more like an ace. "I forgot to ask,"
he explained once, "whether it was ace high,
and when I cut the deck the first time,
I palmed the top card. Any time you get

a chance to take out a little insurance,
never hesitate. I mean, the man was clearly
a Kentuckian, you could tell by the way
he sat his horse, the first time they rode up."

He laughed and readjusted his cane pole.
"Been just my luck, if I'd asked him,

he would have said it was ace low.
That's how we used to play down at Cairo.

So I showed him the six. Either way,
he probably had half the deck up his sleeve.
You know how those Kentuckians are. You
can't trust 'em, even when they're standing

right in front of you." I was just a boy,
eight or nine years old, leaning against
a rusty girder, listening to old Barnabas
half talking to himself, half entertaining me

with his war stories. But I can still recall
looking downriver, on those bright afternoons,
when a sudden wind might come up, rippling
the trees and turning everything to silver,

and I remember thinking that at such moments
I could almost see those cards blowing away—
watch them scattering down the tunnel and on
through the cracks in those boards: see them

tumbling and falling through the air toward
the water, showing one last hand—queens
and eights and a one-eyed jack—and then
landing on the water and disappearing there—

all except this one card my great-grandfather
had kept with him, all these years, that I
could hold in my hand, and touch, and feel
the softness of, while he told the story again.

It was that card that was buried with him,
finally, in an inner pocket of his black suit,
along with his ball pistol, and a turnip watch
on a gold chain that turned out to be brass—

a watch he always said never did work anyhow
but which he had borrowed, from a friend,
years before, without really intending to,
in case Old Fly never found his way back home.

Visit

Whatever day you choose, rain will be falling
out of that granite sky. Whatever path
you take will make no sound. A lone bird calling
through the double row of hemlocks seems half
silenced by the gathering mist. Within,
the house is still, and someone takes your coat
and shows you through the rooms. Here she had been
a child, then a woman, one who scribbled notes
on scraps of butcher paper. Here is her room—
the paisley shawl across the bed, the desk—
and here, in a closet opened for you now,
one of her muslin dresses. In the rain's gloom
you study the shape of the sleeves, the neck,
the bodice and the slim waist. You know how

but not why. For that, go back to the hall
where earlier you saw an old map of the town
a bird's-eye view, in steep perspective, all
shown at a glance—and shrink yourself down
not to that scale but to that time, that place:
pasture and meadow surround the house, trees
shade every path, all things move at the pace
of the sun. Suddenly, skirt hiked to her knees,
shoes kicked aside, she begins to run through
the hayfield, through deep grass, laughing,
calling to others behind her—a loon's cry,
a fierce joy! Gradually coming into view,
her father and older brother go by, passing
without a word. You begin to understand why.

Follow her now, as she leaves the house, climbs
into a carriage, ready to spend a year
at Mount Holyoke Seminary. The times
are troubling: a Baptist preacher spies fear

in the Book of Daniel, the faithful advance
to rooftops for the World's End, Shaker girls
babble in strange tongues while elders prance
on mountainsides. Amid the smoke and swirl
of anti-slavery politics and talk of war
in Mexico, she takes tea with the headmistress,
who explains: Sunday nights in the main hall
the student body assembles; on the floor
a minister chalks a line. Each will profess
her sins and her depravity, then all

will sing hosannas as each passes over
to be saved. The year progresses in this way;
two hundred girls burning with the fever
of salvation cross the line. Then comes a day
in March, when the strange one, Emily
Dickinson, stands alone at the last meeting,
facing them all. Miss Lyon's "family"
huddles in the bleak hall, rain sleeting
the windows, and one iron stove, banked low.
Swaying back and forth in the shifting gloom
above her head, four brassbound lamps cast
quavering light. Something begins to grow
in that unsteadiness—a constancy, a doom
stronger than all their pieties. And lasts.

A poet's life is simply told: the task
of waiting, and of writing down; and listening,
while the visitors come and go. They bask
in talk, and laughter; she sees a glimmering
in the hallway mirror. Rather than a master,
she comes to know herself. In the long days
of silence, and solitude, nothing faster
than her pen inches across the page—stays
for a moment—moves on. A clock chimes.
She rises, goes down to the kitchen to check
the bread baked earlier that morning. Feels

it's cooled enough. Rain by evening. Lines
the basket with a clean white cloth, stacks
the brown loaves inside. Their fragrance heals.

The house and grounds become her world: the path
out through the apple trees, the summer porch,
the upstairs room from which to watch the last
friend, waving goodbye; or the faint torch
flickering out, to mark the holiday's end
on the village common. Not growing old,
she simply dematerializes, sends
the best part away, hides it under folds
of linen in the basket, or in the desk.
When there was music in the drawing room,
she listened from the top of the stairs;
when the house was quiet again, the risk
remained—to have no presence, to assume
all, everything, to be lighter than air.

But can we know such things, or is it true
the face you thought you saw in the glass assumed
a shape you wanted to see—your own? And who
or what she was, and whether she still presumes
on days like this to drift on down the stairs,
staying a room or two ahead, lifting the hem
of her dress, making no sound, as though air
were what she fed on—all that grows dim
in the evening shadows. Whatever remains,
whatever you hoped to find by coming here
(the path through the meadow, the lone bird's
cry, the shawl on the bed) is dark with rain.
Now you must go. What's lost will reappear—
will come back even stronger. In her words.

Recollections of a Contingent of Coxey's Army
Passing through Straughn, Indiana, in April of 1894

> More than 2,500,000 men walked the streets in search
> of work in the terrible winter of 1893-94. . . . It was only
> when government failed to act that angry men began to
> take matters into their own hands.
>
> In Massillon, Ohio, Jacob S. Coxey set about
> organizing a massive march on Washington. . . . On Easter
> Sunday . . . 100 men set out for the Capitol, accompanied
> by half as many reporters. . . . No less than seventeen
> armies set out for Washington in the spring of 1894.
>
> HAROLD U. FAULKNER, *Politics, Reform and*
> *Expansion: 1890-1900*

There by the rail fence in that lost, broken light, that moment
still wavering like a loose ribbon: whether she remembers most
the sound of their singing, or their march through the wagon ruts,
the angry crowd, the elm trees with their great curved branches—

"They cain't be for Coxey, he done got killed a long time ago!"
somebody called out. She remembered it was cold, she could see
her breath, how scared she became when her brothers threw rocks,
how her father cuffed them, while the marshal waved back the crowd—

and on they came, in ragged double file along the National Road,
none of them in step, some reaching to take an apple or a crust
of bread held out for them. It was the first time she recalled
seeing black skin—a man, striding along, paying them no mind—

and in this way they slogged on past the store-fronts and taverns,
past the young doctor reined in and saluting—near the station
a preacher waving his hat, then running to heave a brick at them—
finally only children still following, pretending they had joined—

until they drew abreast of the Tipton place, with its stone wall,
the last house in town, only bare fields ahead of them now—
and she saw a stack of hedgeapples, sheltered by the stones,
that had lasted the winter, and hurried over to gather some—

made an apron with her skirt, as her grandmother had taught her,
and ran along the main road, calling after them until someone
looked around—a gray-haired man in a faded blue coat with badges
on the lapels, tarnished buttons, one arm pinned at the shoulder—

who with his left hand took the sodden green fruit she held out,
stuffing his pockets, nodding gravely, saying nothing she could
remember in later years, but finally reaching down to press
her fingers, then hurrying on, turning back once to wave to her.

Spirea

Then she came, the sybil, out through the doors
of The Bell, the single drinking establishment
permitted in that narrow little country town—
she came out neither staggering nor collapsing
but gliding—not carefully, one step at a time,
like a tight-rope walker, but recklessly, wantonly,
as someone oblivious to danger, who knows already
what lies ahead, and has nothing to fear.
                                        Down
the wooden steps of the board walkway, on down
into the dust and refuse of the street, the rinds
and horse droppings, and they watched her go
without really noticing—since they saw this
every evening, now that warm weather had come,
when she ventured out to wander in the town—
and the fact that she was barefooted, that
she wore only a blue shirtwaist, that her hair
hung the length of her back, and was never combed
or pinned up, that she seldom stopped talking
to herself, that all her relatives were dead,
that she had no place to stay, owned nothing,
needed nothing, harmed no one—
                                        these facts
were accepted, known throughout the community,
were discussed by the ladies' aid society,
by the minister and by the township trustee,
and yet none of them could contain her—not
the bartender, who told her when it was time
to leave, not the old rag buyer, who reined in
his horse, when he saw her, and called to her,
asking her to come sit beside him in the wagon,
and he would take her home—for none of them
would she turn back, even when they pleaded
and called out her name.

Each time she went forth,
when she walked through the streets, the alleys,
in the twilight, some of them encountered her—
the husbands out watering their lawns, the wives
with their children, the young people pausing,
at the corner, with their bicycles, watching her,
seeing her go by. Many avoided her passing;
many were afraid, unable to return her bright gaze.
A light shone from her eyes. Something glimmered
when she moved. There was about her a presence,
an immanence, that announced a way, a direction
most of them could not imagine, would never know.
She walked on, heedless, muttering to herself,
leaving them far behind.
                        In this way she journeyed
through the summer evenings, and into the night,
while all around her doors were closing, lamps
were dimmed, the world was preparing for sleep.
Always she moved in a straight line, pausing
for no obstacle, respecting no property line—
through backyards, over fences, across gardens,
managing to steer, nightly, by a different star—
by Venus smoldering low above the line of trees,
by Mars or Saturn in stark opposition to the moon—
by whatever brightness seemed most beckoning,
however faint or furious its glow.
                        In this way
she traversed all points of the town, stopping
sometimes to speak to whomever or whatever
she encountered—whether house, tree, horse
or child—but invariably moving on, walking
on through the streets and into the countryside,
walking out among the fields, the gravel roads,
walking until she collapsed against a stone wall,
under a hedge, or in a barn, with rain falling,
walking until she lost her way among dark dreams.

In this manner, on the first evening in May, drawn
by an unknown star, she leaves the tavern, and comes
eventually to the edge of town, to the side yard—
to the croquet court, actually—of a professor
of physics at the college, who nightly sets up
his reflecting telescope: and who on this evening
has trained it on an elusive entity—

                        a nebula
thousands of light years away, a great star cluster
tilted on one side, displaying vast spiral arms—
it is this same man, this professor, who notices,
behind him, something struggling through the hedge,
through the arms of the spirea called "bridal-veil,"
through that pale maze of blossoming, that thicket
of lush, damp, drooping, spiraling white branches—
not far away in the twilight he hears someone
coming toward him, then recognizes this wanderer
from the town—

                  watches her shoulder aside the canes,
bursting at last onto the level lawn, then stopping,
righting herself, reaching to touch and feel the welts
along her arms, her shoulders, the thin red cut,
on her cheek—observes her peer about, slowly,
at the house, the arbor, the herbs in their ladder,
her gaze turning at last to the well-dressed man
with his celluloid collar, his knotted silk tie,
where he stands with one hand on the telescope.

Is he young, and handsome, is this semester
his first in the town, has he only recently
accepted a position at the little college?
Does he turn the heads of the young ladies,
does he sing bass in the Baptist church choir,
is he one of the town's leading bachelors?
Or is he a white-haired gentleman, stooped,
round-shouldered, has he been there for years,
taught generations of young people, outlived

an affectionate wife, sent forth children,
lived to see grandchildren, does he reside alone
at the edge of town, on a wide brick street,
in a gas-boom mansion with a massive hedge
of spirea enclosing the property on three sides,
a front gate of cast iron tipped with arrowheads?
Does it matter now whether he is young or old?
Does he know himself about any of these things,
on a night like this, at the moment she emerges
from the spirea's whiteness, as though swum up
through a heavy, pounding surf?
                                          Her shirtwaist
is torn, she is hardened by incessant walking
and wandering, by being out in all weathers,
her breasts and her gaunt body have emerged
androgynous and gleaming, she is aglow now,
dusted with shattered blossom as though prepared
for some elusive ritual, and as she gazes at him
she continues to mutter, to murmur—has in fact
never ceased to speak, to utter strange syllables;
whether she understands the words, he cannot tell.

He waits beside the telescope—the gleaming shaft
poised on its tripod—which earlier he pointed
up into the wealth of stars—earlier, alone,
far from the interference of artificial light,
he had come out, he had set up the equipment,
he carried chalkboard in hand for observations—
he began to search, to locate, to gaze into
the huge glimmering hearth of the night sky—

and only moments ago he had found it, had
checked his coordinates, had seen distinctly—
he had looked up and into, looked out far
toward those myriad outflung arms, that turning,
that vast, still, immeasurable unfolding—

and the visitor, strangely silenced now, begins
to come his way, across the fresh-cut grass—
she approaches, strides toward him unhesitant
and unafraid, reaches to touch the viewing aperture,
already in perfect focus, smiles, and leans down—
fragments of white blossom, living particles
of sundered veil cling to her long hair, drip
from her forearms, her rough hands—she sees,
she looks for a long time. There is no sound
except her slight breathing.
                              Finally she begins,
she raises her head, the light is in her eyes,
the shining, and she speaks what comes. He bows
as though in prayer, knowing there is no difference—
it is the far galaxy, great orb and afterimage
in his brain, it is the milk-white hedge cresting
all around them, it is the unsummoned presence
come at last, and always, up through the waves,
it is the voice speaking through all, to all,
here, now, in the darkness, in the starlight.

Picking Stone

> Speak your latent conviction, and it shall be
> the universal sense; for the inmost in due time
> becomes the outmost. . . . we recognize our
> own rejected thoughts: they come back to us
> with a certain alienated majesty.
>
> *Emerson, "Self-Reliance"*

1

Up north, along the east shore of the lake,
they grow apples, and all kinds of cherries.
Each spring, when the men go out to plow
for asparagus or corn, they find rocks
that had not been there before, boulders
worked up from the earth during the winter,
a harsh crop of stone rising in the furrows.

2

On spring evenings farmers lead their families
past the bare, twisted trees, to go pick stone
while the light is still good. They spread out
across the fresh-turned earth, following
a flatbed truck, searching with their hands
through the broken clods, grasping, struggling,
helping each other heave up what they find.

3

The two older boys, still in baseball uniforms
from a game at the Legion, take turns driving.
Each fills the pockets of his windbreaker
with bits of worked stone—points, scrapers,
tools that have lain underground all this time—
that their grandfather taught them to recognize.
They keep them in cigar boxes under the bed

4

and seldom take them out anymore. Now,
they give the best stones to the smaller sister,
who walks with the old man, who wants to do
what he says, follow where he goes. The father
moves back and forth, now down on his knees
with a son, brushing sand from a boulder,
deciding they will come back and get it

5

with the tractor, now carrying the baby
for a while, suddenly handing it to his wife
and going to help the oldest daughter, who
has lifted a rock and hugs it to her body,
staggering, as though she were burdened
with grief. While he works, while he moves
from one group to another, he looks beyond

6

the trees, across the land's swell, at the lake,
that is vast and unblemished and still,
gleaming with evening light. All winter
it has waited like a great slab of granite,
giving off its hoarded warmth to the land
at the lake's edge, to the roots and the sap
waiting beneath the snow. Now the lake

7

is cold, and will stay that way till summer.
Thunderheads will come from the west,
snapping off branches, bringing the warmth.
At night, if he were not too tired to dream,
the farmer would see the lake, know it to be
the same stone he has lifted all these years,
that he cannot put down, nor hand to another.

8

Hurrying along, he senses that a storm
is gathering north of Old Mission point.
His daughter, who dropped to her knees
when he tried to help her, who let the stone
roll away, who walks now, angry, alone,
across the rows with the wind in her hair—
his daughter knows when they have a load

9

the two boys will drive it south of the barn
and dump it against the pile. That is what
bewilders her: the craggy pile of rocks
at the far end of the barnyard, where she
and her brothers have climbed and played,
that has always been there. Though they add
new rocks each spring, it never seems to change,

10

growing neither smaller nor larger. It is
the mountain that holds her back, balanced
against her dream of leaving the home-place.
Now that she is older, she hates the stones,
hates being taken out to pick them, believes
that whatever weight she adds to the pile
falls through the earth, creeps underground,

11

rises again, to wear the skin from her fingers.
The grandfather holds her little sister's hand,
he is telling the same story, only this time
it is grandmother who is the stone now.
She is under the earth, she will come back,
she will be unchanged. He walks on, silent.
He lifts nothing now. The land and the lake

12

he once held so close their shadows fell
between his own body and hers, as they slept—
that weight has been handed over. Now it is
no heavier than clouds on the horizon, gulls,
wind in the dry grass. Sometimes he thinks
he can hear the older girl slip from the house,
go to meet someone near the pile of stones.

13

steal off to find some place out of the wind.
At other times it's the sound of the wind,
or the memory of being in the barn, years ago,
with the girl from the next farm. He thinks
he knows why his granddaughter lifts stones
as though to hurt something inside herself,
unable to accept the dream of things that grow

14

and move about in darkness, and return.
He alone sees how the stones they gather—
straining to fling them into the truck bed—
begin to fade in the last light, changing
to slate, to the lost colors of the lake
before the rain finally sweeps across it.
By nightfall, his sleep will be all these things

15

dreamed together: currents of water and stone,
a rising and a falling. The father calls out
through the sudden wind, they must gather
a full load before going back. They bend
to the earth, searching. The mother turns
to help the sons, who pry with an iron bar
against a great gray rock. They will not quit,

16

they begin to roar as they bear down on it.
Bits of broken stone fall from their pockets,
and the daughter, leaving the smallest child
in the middle of a row, bends to retrieve them.
A curtain of rain sweeps through the far trees.
The baby, left alone, as though distinguishing
dream from darkness, rises to go toward it.

From *A Dance in the Street* | 2012

Prophet Township

Only that it was a place where snow
and ice could seal off whole sections
for half the winter, where the ground—
even when you dug down to it—could not
be budged.
             If you had someone to bury,
you waited for spring thaw. Children
died from diphtheria and scarlet fever,
old-timers came down with pneumonia,
horses reared up suddenly in the barn.

The coffin would be kept in the parlor
for three days and nights. The watchers
took turns. After the funeral, neighbors
helped carry the box up to the attic
or set it out in one of the back rooms
so it would stay cold but not freeze.
Before the men tacked down the lid,
they filled it up the rest of the way
with rock salt. This was a custom
learned from their grandparents—
how to make it through till spring,
how to handle hardship on their own.
But there were times when no one lasted,
fierce winters when the wood gave out,
when there was nothing left to eat,
no hay to pitch out for the stock,
no way to break down through the ice
on the horse trough, or get the pump
working again.
             With no heat, no money
for seed, they knew they had no choice
but to pack up and leave—head back
to town, try to get a stake together,

go somewhere else. They brought along
what they could carry. Everything else
was left behind: piles of old clothes,
root cellar full of empty Mason jars,
strings of peppers tied to the rafters.

This is a long migration, a traveling
back and forth, over many harsh years.
Even now, people move off the land—
realize they're not going to make it,
understand there's no point in trying.
The old farmhouses are stripped clean,
emptied out, made ready for lightning
or for a final warming fire built
in the middle of the parlor floor
by some transient, some jobless family
camped for the night.
                                    Grass grows
knee-high around the pump, the catalpa
holds up its brown and purple flowers.
Wind, searching along the kitchen shelf,
knocks a last jelly glass to the floor.
Soot bleeds from the hole in the wall
where the flue once went in.
                                    By December
if no fire breaks out, cold weather
clamps down. The freeze and thaw
eats at the plaster—spitting out nails,
breathing in dust, over and over—
gnawing it to the marrow.
                                    Now and then
when I drive past one of these places
set back up the lane—doors unhinged,
windows broken out, lilacs choked up,
willow drooping in the side yard—
I'm never in much of a hurry to stop,
poke around.

Sometimes I sit there
in the driveway for a few minutes,
thinking about it, knowing that if I
step up to the front porch, or find
my way through the weeds to the pump,
there will be a slight breath of wind
just ahead of me, something rustling
through the timothy grass.
                              It will pause,
stopping each time I do, waiting
until everything gets quiet again.
I can't catch up with it, or come
face to face with whatever it is.
I can sense only that it's pleased—
by the way it turns, every so often,
to make sure I'm still coming.

Summit

Small towns. A few houses and a general store.
The map might show only one road going through,
but if you keep driving around long enough,
you begin to understand how they're connected.
There are back roads running in all directions.
You just have to get out and look for them.

People living out there have known each other
for a long time. They still have family reunions
in late August, on plank tables under the trees.
Places with names like Hadley, and Springtown,
and Coatesville. Most of them manage to keep
a grain elevator going, maybe a post office.

I'm a real-estate appraiser. These days
I spend a lot of time out looking at farms.
I've got a bunch of good maps in my car;
old ones, too. You don't want to come back
to town and admit you couldn't even find
the place you were looking for. Or got lost.

One day last September I was driving along
a gravel road between Clayton and Hadley, using
an old county map. Up ahead was a little town
called Summit, that had been a flag stop once,
on a spur slanting off from the main line
to Terre Haute. That spur's been gone for years.

Summit was gone, too. But I found it, after
a while, figured out exactly where it had been,
right at the top of a long rise you could see
stretching for miles across the countryside.
Nothing out there now but lots of beans and corn,
blue sky and clouds. Not even fence rows anymore.

You could almost imagine the train heading west,
up that long grade, pouring on the coal, making
for high ground. When it finally pulled in,
and the telegraph man came out for the mail,
there would be a couple of little kids sitting
on the baggage wagon, waving to the engineer.

I walked up to the only place it could have been.
Right there, at the crest of the hill. Somebody
had kept it mowed. There was a strong wind blowing.
I searched around in the grass for a long time,
but I couldn't find anything. Not a trace.
Only the land itself, and the way it still rose up.

Roadside Crosses

This is a state where nothing marks the spot
officially. They crop up now and then
out on the freeway, or in rustic plots
sometimes, near S-curves in the country, when
the corn's knee-high. A cross, or even two
or three, made out of poles or boards, white-
washed or painted. They seem to have a view
of nothing at all, only the blurred lights
of oncoming cars, and the eighteen-wheelers
roaring by. Memory has a harsh sting—
blown back like the fine grit that settles
while you walk here now, no special healer,
merely a friend or brother, stopped to bring
a can of flowers, to place among the nettles.

Fire Burning in a 55-Gallon Drum

Next time you'll notice them on your way to work
or when you drive by that place near the river
where the stockyards used to stand, where everything

is gone now. They'll be leaning over the edge
of the barrel, getting it started—they'll step back
suddenly, and hold out their hands, as though

something fearful had appeared at its center.
Others will be coming over by then, pulling up
handfuls of weeds, bringing sticks and bits of paper,

laying them in gently, offering them to something
still hidden deep down inside the drum.
They will all form a circle, their hands almost

touching, sparks rising through their fingers,
their faces bright, their bodies darkened by smoke,
by flakes of ash swirling around them in the wind.

In the Warehouse District

Once a man I know who deals in pianos and who takes anything
as a trade-in took me to a bricked-up building on a side street

on a day approaching 100 degrees, and with a coat-hanger key
let me inside a shuttered room filled with hundreds of pianos

so crowded together there was no space to walk between them.
All uprights, all damaged—cases nicked and scarred, keys missing—

all worthless and beyond repair. Four cast-iron pillars
stamped with ivy reached up to the corners of a skylight

boarded over with plywood. The lids of the pianos were thick
with soot and chunks of fallen plaster. All I could do was climb up

and walk around on top of them. The dealer stayed in the alley
and smoked a cigarette while I stepped from one dusty frame

to another, up higher than I should have been, going nowhere
in particular, occasionally hearing, beneath my feet, an echo,

a hollow stirring, as though some mechanism, some tension
still surviving, had registered my passing. Now and then I stopped

to kneel, to lean all the way over to an opened keyboard,
halfway expecting to see my own reflection there. Finally

reached down among the missing keys and touched a middle C—
listened to that single note ringing through the darkened room.

In the Military Park

At dawn, near the parade ground,
in the shadow of the obelisk,
where the fountains have not yet
been turned on, you can look out

and see the youthful instructor,
sometimes a man, usually a woman,
following five paces behind the one
who is blind, who is being taught

how to walk with a long, thin cane
that is swept from side to side
across the empty paths. They come
early, there is never anyone else

in the park at this hour. Immediately
after you drive by, you are not sure
you really understood what you saw.
It seems mixed up with something else,

some old, half-remembered story
that comes to you now, at the stoplight—
how she yearned to reach out and take
his hand, how he kept pressing ahead,

beyond the shadows, into the sunlight,
while she fell farther behind, and in
another moment, he will turn, and
there will be nothing, nothing at all.

The Pool at Noon

She is the secretary. She wears a bathing cap
of white rubber, to enclose her brittle hair,
and an elasticized suit of shirred green fabric.
She does not dive into the water, but descends,
backward, down the shaky tubular ladder,
into the shallows, where the water is calm
and strangely luminous, and smells always
of chlorine—
                        the echoes, among high girders
and skylights long ago painted over, of water
lapping in the scum-gutter, of dishes clinking,
far away, in the kitchen—
                                    and everywhere,
across the glazed bottom and sides of the pool,
the shifting reflections and bands of soft light
in endless permutations—
                                    she settles down
amid the ripples, spreads her arms, launches
herself, with her head back, into the stillness,
and begins her slow, symmetric sweeping.

We are in the YMCA of an ancient city
of abandoned mills and red-brick factories
that stretch along the river. This is the pool
built years ago, for the youth of the town,
when there was still some money. These days
the walls are pocked with broken tiles, the pipes
conveying the water are discolored with rust,
but still the elementary children of the town
are bussed here, and taught how to swim
by teen-aged instructors not much older
than themselves.
                        The children are brown
and black and pale white, they are separated

by gender, they swim naked, according to
an old custom, in this high-ceilinged pool
that booms with their squeals, their voices—
although now it is noon, they are dressed
and made to line up. Toting their backpacks,
herded outside, they form circles on the lawn,
and eat their lunch from plastic containers.

Here, in the pool's silence, and the constant
flickering of reflections, is the secretary,
who weekdays at this hour will backstroke
across the still water—
                                    at the other end,
the deep end, is the pool maintenance man,
retired and in his seventies, with flaccid skin
and patches of grizzled hair on his arms
and legs and chest, who receives no pay,
and volunteers his services—
                                    in order that
day after day, in his faded, baggy trunks
and his plastic nose-clip, he can climb up
and walk to the end of the 3-meter board,
and stand for a moment, and then step off
into the sheen of ever-shifting reflections
lining the pool's floor—
                                    he becomes the shaft
of a needle slipped into impermanence,
he is that which almost touches something
balancing in the depths—
                                    he bobs up again,
returns once more to the world of gaskets
and broken tiles and murmuring children.
Reemerging, he floats improbably, since
he lacks bulk, and is nothing more than
a scarecrow, with white hair rayed out
around his head—but he has learned
how to hang motionless, arms extended,

only his face showing—
                              thus the rituals
of these two, who are old acquaintances,
but who do not speak—him suspended,
she progressing slowly across the shallows
with her eyes closed—
                              one moving, the other
drifting, and all around them the silence,
the placid water, the pale tremors of light
endlessly searching and shimmering.

Plastic Sack

Lifted by a warm current, ballooned
for a moment out of the slow swirl
of dust and paper cups blowing along
the alley, this diaphanous plastic bag—

product of modern technology, made
by the billions, the recyclable kind
you get at the checkout, when the clerk
asks you the inevitable question.

Upside down now, strangely inflated,
almost responsive, balanced among gusts
of wind, making no sound, its handles—
dangling loops—somehow reminding me

of snapshots of my father, on the porch,
that first autumn after the war ended,
wearing that slight, mostly forgotten
article of clothing, the undershirt.

But this is no revenant, no survivor
of those days. There are no features
on this face, nothing but a blankness
reflecting the light of the streetlamp

on the corner. It is only a plastic sack,
having come to the end of its journey,
almost aware that something is missing,
managing to rise up for one last look.

Wind Egg

Once a wind egg called out to a young girl who went each morning
to collect eggs for her grandmother—"O child, do not take me,
let the hen my mother set for ten more days, I long to walk about
in the world, even now I can see the horse grazing in the meadow."

"How can this be?" the girl wondered. "Neither white egg nor brown
ever speaks to me. They have nothing to say, in their thin shells,
even when we hold them up to the candle's glow. But this one
has a blue eye, and wears no coat. I had better ask grandmother."

The old woman had peered into hens' eggs for so many years
she could see into the heart of things. When the child told her
of the talking egg, she was not deceived. "It is the wind,"
she declared, "trying to make mischief among honest folk."

"Never could we leave the brood mares alone in the pasture
when the wind blew up from the river. Crossing the barnyard
in winter, I too have felt it, reaching in. An egg without
a shell is an abomination. Cast it out for the hogs to eat!"

That night the girl dreamt of an empty nest, and a blue eye
singing to itself. She reached out to take it in her hand
but it was like holding water. She threw it against the wall
and it slid down and became whole again, balanced in her palm.

"No," she said to herself next morning, and she opened the pocket
of her apron and slipped in the strange egg. The black hen cackled,
and the rooster crowed. "Alas, I can see nothing!" the egg called,
but the girl's thighs kept it warm, and in nine days it quickened.

Lying alone in her room, she awoke to the glint of a new moon
shining through the window, and there was no membrane, no shell,
no barrier to what she could become. Next morning, the old woman
looked away from the tremor of light into which she was gazing.

"Go," she said, "for nothing can keep you here now. That is the way
of the wind—it is always blowing, always wanting to be elsewhere."
She turned back to her candle. "I long to be out in the world,"
the young woman said. "The horse waits for me in the meadow."

The horse galloped toward her through the tall grass, and the wind
leapt from her apron, into its sleek body, its churning hooves.
The horse shuddered, and knelt down, and she mounted up.
"Let us ride," said a clear voice that was all around her now.

Hidden Door

The old stories do not end the way you were told.
Hansel and Gretel do not escape from the witch's house;
they decide to stay. Ali Baba does not emerge from the cave
but enters a subterranean chamber that goes on for miles.

At every juncture there is always a hidden door.
When the characters step through, they enter a realm
having little resemblance to the world the rest of us know.
The old stories are never about what happens next,

but about the glass vial on the table. After days of heat,
you hear three sharp raps, and look out and see
winter hurrying through the forest—not rain or snow,
but a wind stripping the leaves and stiffening the grass.

Cicadas in the Rain

Only when it began to rain could I hear it,
in late summer, after they had all risen high
in the saucer magnolia tree—a soft, slow rain
at first, while the light still held in the west.

That sound so familiar, so unhesitant, but never
during a storm, and yet with drops plashing
and pelting through the leaves, their voices
coalesced in ways I had never heard before—

some strange harmonic of summer's ending,
some last reinforcement or challenge—mounting
against the rain's insistence, trying to outdo it,
seeking a pulse within the larger immensity,

and succeeding, as though a door had opened,
and I heard pure sound issuing forth, stately
and majestic, even golden, while all around it,
darkness, rain falling, trees bent by the wind.

Sphinx

It lives on, and with each new day, asks
the old questions, of strangers passing by,
or even of itself. Often I have heard it
calling across the wastes, like a hot wind
that brings no relief, that sorts through
acres of sand, dust, shards, broken stones,
finding nothing. Out of Egypt it came,
aeons ago, to stand at the crossroads
while travelers, in the distance, approach.

Oedipus spoke with it, though that exchange
is lost, and all manner of false stories
sprung up in later years. Of all myths,
all tales, it is the most ancient and remote,
the most elemental. Each time it appears,
like some presence that casts no shadow,
it is the wayfarer whose life has changed,
not the Sphinx, which is outside history,
and uncaring, like the oldest of sibyls.

Each time you hear its muttered questions
they strike you in a different way, though
whether you go on two legs, or four,
or three, is of little consequence now.
Rather, you must continue along the path
through rocky places, over drifted sands,
past steep ascents rising to the mountains.
The Sphinx at such moments walks beside you,
neither leading nor following, asking
or answering. It has sojourned here before,
and watches to see which way you will turn.

War

In Goya's "Disasters of War," print
after print of huddled women, already
raped, beaten, defeated, struggling
to bring a cup of water to another—

hillsides draped with bodies of the dead,
a priest tied to a stake, darkness,
stones, illumination within that world
always stark, unforgiving, wild—

yet in scene after scene the backgrounds
begin to dominate, the fierce stippling
and cross-hatching that never seems
to repeat itself, and is always different

from one print to the next—the void,
the emptiness, that we see swirling
and drifting about in the images
of Dürer, Rembrandt, Van Gogh—

quantum vacuum, beyond the limits
of the imagination, but shown, particles
popping into existence, screaming
on a frequency we cannot pick up—

and yet perfectly composed, balanced,
this darkness, this light that Goya bestows
on these huddled figures, these creatures
with bat wings, poring over their ledgers.

At the Art Institute

Once when I was in Chicago
up on the second floor
of the Art Institute, looking
at all the Impressionists
and the post-Impressionists
and the Fauves and the Cubists,
there was this man pushing
his mother in a wheelchair.

Now and then, under his breath,
he called her "Mother."
He pushed her right up
to every painting in the room,
and read from the placard
as though announcing
departures and arrivals
in some busy air terminal—
the title of this particular work,
the years during which
the artist lived, the painting's
place in the history of art,
the medium, and the year
of acquisition.
                    Slowly, patiently,
from one painting to the next,
he guided the creaking machine,
placing her squarely in front
of each canvas, then beginning
to read aloud in a nasal whine.
Other patrons in the room
stared and shook their heads.

Within those huge frames
the world of La Belle Époque

blazed with sudden color
and patches of dappled light,
while the names themselves
came back like a lost litany—
Renoir and Manet, Pissarro,
Sisley, Monet, and Degas—
all mispronounced, all
strangely transformed
by his harsh calling out.

The woman in the wheelchair
ignored the others in the room.
Her eyes were hooded, her body
gnarled and shrunken—

                              she gripped
the tubular metal armrests
and peered up at the paintings
while her son recited the names
and reeled off the explanations.

So on they labored, backward
through the nineteenth century,
finally entering the precincts
of the salon painters, the creators
of *les grandes machines,* of early
Puvis de Chavannes and late
Bougereau—vast historical
and mythological compositions
that filled entire walls—the light
in those frames becoming more dim
and muddy with each step he took,
each turn of the creaking wheels
on the contraption in which
he pushed her along—

                              he continuing
to bark out the words, but neither
of them really seeing the paintings

any longer, both of them caught up
in something they insisted on
accomplishing, some witnessing
that overwhelmed them now,
some courage or indomitability
or reprise of moment long ago—

and in this manner they passed
from view, down the hallways
and through the long corridors,
until I could hear them no more.

Mourning Dove Ascending

At the moment of rising, when it takes flight
through the clearing, in the false light of dawn,
the notes of its call stay with you—a sound

you have been drawn toward all of your life,
without knowing why. Something in that voice
still has the power to summon, even as it fades,

even as the creature's wings begin to make
a different kind of music—an elusive whistling
that spreads in circles and in overlapping waves.

It is a sound more rare, more hushed than song,
issuing not from the throat but the body,
the body working against time and space,

finding purchase, trusting in the outcome
of that endeavor—the whisper and whirl
of the feathers, the vanishing into the dark.

Up in Michigan

How do we know when it's God?
Dan Wakefield

In what way do we encounter the holy?
How do we know it to be genuine?
A friend told me once of being on top
of another man's wife, and noticing
something cold and sharp set against
the bridge of his nose. Even in the dark
he knew it had the heft of a shotgun.
"Double-barreled, twelve-gauge,"
someone said. Two hammers clicked.
Awaken now, the dream recedes.

A light switched on. When his pupils
adjusted, he could look all the way up
both barrels, as though peering into
two long, metallic tunnels, and see
far away, like stars, the paper wadding
of each shell, bunched up, crimped,
ready to enter his skull. Louder now,
the husband, verging on incoherence,
asking him, over and over, why?
From a great distance, someone beckons.

I think it would be like that. It could be
no other way. You would know this was
the thing itself. That you were suddenly
in the presence of the ultimate. My friend
explained that he tried to focus on the voice
and its terrible immediacy, but by the smell,
he realized his sphincters had given way,
his bladder had emptied, he had lost control

156

of everything except this great need to listen.
Come near, I have something to tell you.

Strangely, at that moment, he remembered
his father, dead on the gurney, wrapped in
loose green scrubs, only his face showing,
the vitality gone, the retreat into nothingness
begun—but supremely peaceful, as though
something he had encountered, sacred
and unnamable, all of his life, had finally
revealed itself. As though he had heard
the voice, and at last come face to face.
All that was but prelude to this moment.

And the solution? With no way out,
both barrels pressed between his eyes,
his loins soured by his own excrement,
"somehow I managed to talk to him,"
he told me, years later. "I kept on talking,
until he put it down. He had tossed her
across the room. She got up, made coffee.
I managed to get my clothes on. I left.
I never saw either one of them again."
Flat stones skipping across the water.

But he had gone back, once, to the house,
a cabin on a steep bluff, on the west edge
of Torch Lake. It was abandoned, slipped
from its moorings, tilted toward the water.
"There was nothing left. Biker magazines.
Coffeepot. Porcupines find a way to get in.
They need salt, they gnaw anything touched
by humans. Broom handles, wooden spoons,
clothes pins. Chewed down, eaten away."
The widening circles merge, then disappear.

Blank Paper

Those pieces of paper—not the news clippings,
the Valentine bookmarks, the stamped envelopes—
but the blank pieces, sometimes two or three sheets
of heavy bond, and not always the same size,
as though they had been cut down carefully,
or trimmed for some special purpose—those sheets
of watermarked paper I run across in used books
in the secondhand store near the bus station,
or in the old shop the rare-book dealer's widow
still keeps open, on a side street, two days a week,
though he is gone, and the rent so high these days—

All these years I have been finding such sheets
but not been able to read them, not understand
how their blankness, their peculiar emptiness,
has always been there, tucked within those pages,
balancing the weight of the words and letters,
waiting to offer a certain clarity or freedom
to any stranger who might run across them.

I have a friend who lives out west, who dates
from the days of the Santa Fe Super Chief
and Fred Harvey's restaurants, and hours spent
in dusty hotel lobbies, waiting to close a sale.
Sometimes he writes on stationery taken
from the night tables in single rooms, stacks
of paper placed there beside the Gideons' Bible,
in the drawer that never contains anything else.

Mornings, he stops at the newsstand on the square,
and buys a chromolithographed postcard showing
the memorial hospital in Atchison, Kansas,
or the boyhood home of William Jennings Bryan.
It is all blank, everything he collects, and when
he writes, he really has nothing to say. Sometimes

he simply sends empty sheets, with the letterhead
showing the façade of the New Excelsior Hotel,
or all the trucks lined up in front of the creamery.

We both know this is big country, it is replete
with empty spaces. There are people, everywhere,
who take out a few pieces of paper, maybe it is
expensive paper, they have been saving it, now
they are going to sit down and write to someone,
and say things they have always wanted to say.
But it has been a long time since they have written
anything at all, and they need a pen, they get up
to go look for one, and suddenly the phone rings—
so they slip the sheets of paper inside a book.

Do I have a gift for finding such things, years
after the fact? No, my doing so is accidental,
I am a simple man, prone to the same delays
and uncertainties as anyone else. I too began
with the best of intentions. There were truths
I dreamed of writing once, that would come
from the heart, that would make a difference.
But other things came first. My own books
began to harbor odd pieces of blank paper.

Even now, up in the attic, inside old volumes
I cannot bring myself to throw away, I find
such sheets—cream-colored and deckle-edged,
made in the last century out of discarded rags
and strips of linen.
                        And I think, yes, it is better
that they remain here, slipped among these pages.
In this way they can still offer a new beginning;
they might even be put to advantage someday.
I still believe this can happen. I still imagine
such discoveries are possible—the way light
from a lone window reaches into this corner
and manages to show these forgotten shapes.

Under the Snowball Bush

Let him crawl which yet lies sleeping
Through the deep grass of the meadow!
Shelley

Look not under the lilacs, with their lavender blossoms, their white,
   that stand like thickets along both sides of the garden path,
      their canes so rich, so laden, you can barely pass through;

No, nor below the spring-house, where the late wisteria clings
   to the rocks in the limestone wall, where long clusters
      of blue flowers spill down and pool in the shadows;

No, nor within the shaggy tunnel of spirea bordering the side yard,
   the spangled hedge that leans heavily now, that droops
      almost to the ground, to the scattering of violets there;

Nor among clumps of peonies lining the driveway, nor the mock orange,
   nor the clematis inching up to shade the front-porch swing,
      nor the honeysuckle nodding in a breeze that promises rain;

Not even in the pale dark of the apple tree, by the summer kitchen,
   that has lost half its branches, and leans now, propped up
      with a board, its flowers chalk white against a slate sky;

Look not in any of those places, where things open at last to the wind,
   sending their sweetness to mingle with the smell of cut grass,
      with the odor of damp earth spaded and turned in the garden.

Look instead along the front walk, not quite to the wrought-iron fence,
   near the row of maples, where you can see the road from town,
      and the turn-off to the river, and there you will find

The place that I mean: under the snowball bush, where the grass
    is adrift with falling petals, where the white tomcat—
        the long-haired stray, with one brown eye and one blue—

Sleeps in the shadows. If you waken him, he will rise stiffly
    and step through the dappled light, stretching before you
        on the flagstones, first the front legs, then the back;

But you must help him, for he cannot remember the way. Asleep now,
    is he the wind unraveling, or simply another row of whiteness
        raked by the wind? Is he rain receding, or rain approaching?

You have only to reach out and take a branch, and shake it, slowly,
    carefully, so that the blossoms loosen from their bolls,
        so that they drift down and cover him in his dreaming.

Snow

At every hand there are moments we
cannot quite grasp or understand. Free

to decide, to interpret, we watch rain
streaking down the window, the drain

emptying, leaves blown by a cold wind.
At least we sense a continuity in

such falling away. But not with snow.
It is forgetfulness, what does not know,

has nothing to remember in the first place.
Its purpose is to cover, to leave no trace

of anything. Whatever was there before—
the worn broom leaned against the door

and almost buried now, the pile of brick,
the bushel basket filling up with thick,

gathering whiteness, half sunk in a drift—
all these things are lost in the slow sift

of the snow's falling. Now someone asks
if you can remember—such a simple task—

the time before you were born. Of course
you cannot, nor can I. Snow is the horse

that would never dream of running away,
that plods on, pulling the empty sleigh

while the tracks behind it fill, and soon
everything is smooth again. No moon,

no stars to guide your way. No light.
Climb up, get in. Be drawn into the night.

What Is Dream?

What is dream, ultimately, but a testing
of darkness, a venture out into that world,
the bourne from which no traveler returns?
I heard two voices from the deep. The first,
"Is he betrayed, are night and permanence
unmoored, so that the shifting sense seems right,
and nothing stays?" The other quick to answer,
"Boundless this voyage, as to the farthest star
this heading, midst the stellar silence, yet
a thousand thousand times, and still he glides,
encountering nothing." "It is well. Each dream
is but a childish step apart from all
familiarity or face. The void
that will be his eternally takes on
a pleasant guise, and seems a touch away,
almost within his grasp." *And softly said,*
dear heart, how like you this? So they spoke on,
and by the dawn that broke—the even light
that came into the room—the dream dispelled,
and I was back once more amid the sound
of wakening birds and wind-beguiling trees.

New Poems

Clouds

I would like to rise within one
    as though unbound—
Bodiless, but not withdrawn from
    the endless round

Of circumambient winds. I would
    be vaporous, yet
Show texture clear, as in driftwood
    or empty net.

My shadow, far below, would seem
    content to go
Across the green fields like a dream
    of April snow.

Schoolhouse

What were you seeking when the door
    held by one hinge
Came loose, and toppled to the floor?
    What of the fringe

Of scattered bricks? Yet still it stands,
    near the far edge
Of the woods. The pump's iron bands
    grip the stone ledge.

Where the playground was, not a trace
    of footsteps now.
Only the drifts of Queen Anne's lace
    curtsy and bow.

Dryad

At first the light encrypted there
    when you stepped out
Into the mist—the windswept hair,
    the swirling rout

Of leaves—was held back by the stark
    and tangled names
That must take on a colder spark
    before they flame.

But when you spoke in runes, the choir
    of leaves was stilled
And all the trees became a fire
    of darkness spilled.

Awakening

Not sleep at all, that from our eyes
    we brush away
In those first moments, nor surprise
    the night's array

Of dreams has vanished with the dawn.
    Rather, the sense
That something not quite touched is gone.
    Intelligence

Most rare still lingers in the glass—
    that strange demeanor,
Those flowers momentarily passed
    by some dark gleaner.

Homestead

So small. Now that I've come again,
    I still don't know
How all of us could fit within.
    Rain turned to snow,

Cicadas in a leafy year—
    the time went by
So slowly then. Nothing to fear
    that only I

Stand here today, at last grown tall,
    returned—almost
Forgetful now, yet seeing all.
    Even this ghost.

Gone

The five-string banjo that he played
    throughout the night
Stands propped against the balustrade,
    no one in sight.

At times I thought I halfway sensed
    what music meant
To him. But not today. Silence,
    like something pent

For years, wells up within this ring
    of fretted trees,
While wind explores new fingerings
    among the leaves.

Web

Tattered, it still shows her caress
    in strands that run
And stretch about an emptiness—
    where now the sun

Illumines them, as though a wheel
    had come unhinged
From some god's golden car, to reel
    upon the wind

And melt away. No matter where
    he looks, there will
Be only absence caught by air
    grown richer still.

Etruria

How long ago? When even glass
    did not exist,
When our two faces seemed to pass
    within a mist

Of polished bronze. That ancient name
    of Tuscany
Almost forgotten, yet the flame
    that I can see

Within the mirror, captured there—
    the pins you took,
One by one, from your auburn hair.
    That pensive look.

Boleyn

Surely she knew. From that window
    one still looked out
While her recession wound below
    without a shout

Or murmur, calm and clear as on
    a summer's day.
As when, revealed at last, you turn
    your level gaze

Unto the other. That knowing
    stays forever—
What time's imperious mowing
    cannot sever.

Vow

Now, by that dark entanglement
    in which we knew
That neither time nor space had lent
    dimension to

Our souls entwined—so that, unspooled
    and distant, we
Would ever be attuned, and schooled
    invisibly,

Each to the other bound—by this
    I swear. And who
Conveys the stars will know this kiss
    proves us both true.

Cross-harp

Something about her seemed suffused
    with other days;
A thousand times I'd heard the blues
    but not this way.

As though somewhere near Pontchartrain
    she'd caught the sound
The barges make, or that freight train
    that comes around

When you're not listening, and blows
    the moment back
Again. When only green light shows
    along the track.

Torc

That twisted silver on her wrist
    I recognize,
But not the neck, whose final twist
    closed both her eyes.

What dreams we would betray, what days
    of sacrifice
Perpetuate, until we say
    this will suffice—

This beauty slain—so gods, appeased,
    do us no harm.
And for our sins, this bracelet eased
    upon her arm.

Ariadne

It's not a labyrinth, I said,
    more like a maze
That opens circles in your head
    until the daze

Of noon has vanished, and you hear
    the hollow tread
Of some hoofed creature drawing near.
    Give me the thread,

He said impatiently, I have
    kingdoms to win,
And more than schoolgirls to save.
    I pushed him in.

Poetry

Such music will not come again
    until some voice,
Enraptured, takes the words, and then
    not quite by choice

Breathes into them that holy fire
    of paradigm
And passion sweetly joined. The spire
    endures, outlined

Against the far horizon. He
    who would perceive
The window's blaze of rose must be
    down on both knees.

Perseus

Not you—that began whispering
    when I drew near,
Bright blade in hand, intercepting
    and showing clear

Your face, gleaming on the surface
    of my shield, right
Become left—but a sibilance
    drawn bowstring tight

Issuing from your writhing hair.
    Then backward I
Whirled and struck, darkening the air
    with all those sighs.

Twilight

As fireflies, like vials of flame,
    break and refill
Their slender flasks, and as the name
    of crickets still

Concatenates against the dark—
    let me retain
A measure of each drifting spark,
    each silver chain,

To savor in some colder world
    when summer's done—
In verse, and like illustrious pearls,
    each moment strung.

Question

Wind, what is it that you hold most
     sacred? I would
Answer your call, and seek the ghost
     in the dark wood,

The tilted stones, but you rush on,
     remote, uncaught,
Averse to the nightingale's song
     that ever sought

To draw you close. And long I have
     kept vigil, wind,
While you searched through the starry cave,
     finding no end.

Polyxena

Achilles, though in stringent death
    you seized on me
To grace your tomb, with my last breath
    I fervently

Revealed, to all the Argive host
    assembled there,
What you would never touch. At most,
    in this place where

We two are shades, your reaching out
    to take my wrist
Finds only echoes of their shout
    within the mist.

Graveyard

Neglected for a hundred years
    and yet they say
At dusk the caretaker appears
    to cut the hay

And set the fallen stones upright.
    Where yucca spires
Its pale white clusters into night,
    his ghost inquires

If they will help him with his task?
    Those far below,
Mistaken now for flowers, ask
    that it be so.

Achilles

I to Apollo's temple came
    to pledge my troth,
Polyxena. And yet the aim
    of Paris, wroth

At Hector's degradation, found
    my naked heel.
Still I would have you, underground—
    your death would seal

My funeral rites. Once I was man
    and you were maid,
But when I seek you now my hand
    finds only shade.

Mourning

Now where to turn? And how to leave
    alone upon
The bier what we have come to grieve?
    Some antiphon

Still haunts us, since such melodies
    meant to control
Or fend off sorrow fail to seize
    the moment. Whole,

His life was, while these syllables
    will not outlast
This wilderness intractable
    that holds him fast.

Philoctetes

Know then, Paris, that the arrow,
    like the serpent
Stepped upon, strikes to the marrow.
    Though you repent

Those choices made, that quarrel stirred,
    this dart of mine
Feels no remorse. Achilles heard
    your arrow's whine

And knew it was a mortal sting.
    Eurydice
Stung, too, and nothing he might sing
    would set her free.

Adultery

Although it sometimes happens—wrong
    soon giving way
To might have been—as in the song
    the radio plays

Before I reach to change the dial.
    Don't turn it off,
You say, I like the glow. And while
    we soon enough

Must let it go, it almost seems
    this moment in
A darkened room with you redeems
    what some call sin.

Treadwheel

At first you did not guess, could not
    imagine how
It waited in the shadows. Caught,
    forsaken now,

You were encircled, made to climb
    an undertow
That never ceased. Brought there each time
    and pinioned so,

You came to see how that slow grind
    of hidden gears
That lifted you had made you blind
    to all their fears.

Priestess

You, sibyl, elusive taper
    in that bleak house,
Hoarding your scribbles on paper
    like any mouse,

Your secrets safe in a drawer—
    hardly caring
If anyone ever saw or
    thought of sharing

Such treasure. Yet always for you
    the rising fumes
Of the eglantine, the deep blue
    of those dark rooms.

Moth

By now there will be no return,
      for you have flown
Into that realm where creatures burn
      away, and own

No lasting secrets. Candle's flame
      survives, but you
No longer feel or have a name—
      though once, when new,

You landed on my finger, where
      your moment's stay
Seemed endless, till that other flare
      called you away.

Journeyman

Glances about the shop now. Trays
    of type refilled,
Galley proofs hung to dry. The days
    shorter, the skills

Repetitive. Time to bring out
    the haversack,
Face the long road ahead, the doubt,
    the inner lack,

The still unanswered questions. Ink,
    and how it flows
Sometimes, on its own. Time to think.
    A door to close.

Visitor

Awake again, and now we hear
    what comes by night
Through falling snow, that has no fear
    and would alight

Near where we sleep, among the leaves—
    that may not know
What draws it to this place, that grieves
    and cannot go

Among the hidden things, but stays,
    and by its calling,
Enters into the many ways
    of the snow's falling.

Prescription

The fast ends; soon will come a time
    to feast again.
There is no poetry to chime
    away the sin

Of wanting, or the subtle snare
    of grief. Each has
A portion in that market where
    we hope at last

To show our wares. Drink then, take up
    the poisons earth
Provides, and in that bitter cup
    assay your worth.

Evergreen

Make me, like this tall tree, thy means
    to celebrate,
So that my outward limbs will lean
    against their fate

Of sky and wind and rain. And by
    such natural grace
Let me be formed accordingly—
    new growth apace

With old, a lasting balance kept
    and always green
Between the moment and the debt
    to things unseen.

IN THE TED KOOSER CONTEMPORARY POETRY SERIES

Darkened Rooms of Summer:
New and Selected Poetry
Jared Carter

To order or obtain more information
on this or other University of
Nebraska Press titles, visit
nebraskapress.unl.edu.

OTHER WORKS BY JARED CARTER

COLLECTIONS

A Dance in the Street
Cross this Bridge at a Walk
Les Barricades Mystérieuses
After the Rain
Work, for the Night Is Coming

CHAPBOOKS

Blues Project
Situation Normal
The Shriving
Millennial Harbinger
Pincushion's Strawberry
Fugue State
Early Warning

EBOOKS

Time Capsule
Reading the Tarot